PC Tools Deluxe™ 6 Instant Reference

Gordon McComb

SYBEX ®

San Francisco • Paris • Düsseldorf • Soest

Acquisitions Editor: Dianne King
Series Editor: James A. Compton
Editor: Richard L. Mills
Technical Editor: Avon Murphy
Word Processors: Scott Campbell, Ann Dunn, Lisa Mitchell
Series Book Designer: Ingrid Owen
Desktop Publishing Specialists: Dan Brodnitz, Rina Malonzo
Proofreader, Production Assistant: R. M. Holmes
Indexer: Nancy Anderman Guenther
Cover Designer: Thomas Ingalls + Associates

SYBEX is a registered trademark of SYBEX, Inc.

TRADEMARKS: SYBEX has attempted throughout this book to distinguish proprietary trademarks from descriptive terms by following the capitalization style used by the manufacturer.

SYBEX is not affiliated with any manufacturer.

Every effort has been made to supply complete and accurate information. However, SYBEX assumes no responsibility for its use, nor for any infringement of the intellectual property rights of third parties which would result from such use.

The text of this book is printed on recycled paper.

Copyright ©1990 SYBEX Inc., 2021 Challenger Drive, Alameda, CA 94501. World rights reserved. No part of this publication may be stored in a retrieval system, transmitted, or reproduced in any way, including but not limited to photocopy, photograph, magnetic or other record, without the prior agreement and written permission of the publisher.

Library of Congress Card Number: 90-71220
ISBN: 0-89588-728-2

Manufactured in the United States of America

10 9 8 7 6 5 4 3 2 1

SYBEX INSTANT REFERENCES

We've designed SYBEX *Instant References* to meet the evolving needs of software users, who want essential information easily accessible, in a clear and concise form. Our best authors have distilled their expertise into compact reference guides in which you can look up the precise steps for using any feature, including the available options. More than just summaries, these books also provide insights into effective usage drawn from our authors' wealth of experience.

Other SYBEX Instant References are:

AutoCAD Instant Reference
George Omura

dBASE IV 1.1 Programmer's Instant Reference
Alan Simpson

dBASE IV 1.1 User's Instant Reference
Alan Simpson

DOS Instant Reference
Greg Harvey and
Kay Yarborough Nelson

Harvard Graphics Instant Reference (December 1990)
Gerald Jones

Lotus 1-2-3 Instant Reference, Release 2.2
Greg Harvey and
Kay Yarborough Nelson

Norton Utilities Instant Reference
Michael Gross

WordPerfect 5 Instant Reference
Greg Harvey and
Kay Yarborough Nelson

WordPerfect 5.1 Instant Reference
Greg Harvey and
Kay Yarborough Nelson

Acknowledgments

Many thanks to the SYBEX team, particularly Dianne King, Jim Compton, and Richard Mills, for helping me see this book to completion. It was much harder to do than I thought, but they made the journey a little easier.

Table of Contents

Introduction ix

Part One
PC SHELL

Active List Switch	2
Attribute Change	3
Background Mat	6
Change Drive	7
Change User Level	8
Clear File	9
Compare	11
Compare Disk	11
Compare File	13
Copy	14
Copy Disk	14
Copy File	16
Date/Time	18
Default Viewer	20
Define Function Keys	21
Delete	23
Delete File	23
Directory Maint	25
Directory Sort	31
Disk Info	32
Disk Map	34
DOS Command Line	36
Edit File	37
Exit PC Shell	39

File Display Options	40
File Edit	44
File List Filter	44
File List Window	46
File Map	47
File Select Filter	49
Find	52
Format Data Disk	52
Hex Edit	55
Hex Edit File	55
Hide Windows	58
LapLink/QC	59
Launch	60
Locate File	61
Make System Disk	64
Memory Map	65
Modify Applications List	67
Modify Display	71
More File Info	73
Move	74
Move File	74
One List Display	76
Park Disk	78
Print Directory	79
Print File	79
Print File List	81
Quick File View	82
Quick Run	85
Rename	86
Rename File	86
Rename Volume	87
Re-Read The Tree	88

Reset Selected Files	89
Run	89
Save Configuration	90
Save Configuration File	91
Screen Colors	91
Search Disk	94
Setup Configuration	96
Short Cut Keys	98
Size/Move Window	99
System Info	100
Text Search	102
Tree/Files Switch	107
Tree List Window	108
Two List Display	109
Undelete	110
Undelete Files	111
Unselect Files	113
Verify	114
Verify Disk	114
Verify File	116
View	117
View/Edit Disk	118
Viewer Cfg.	120
View Window	121
Wait On DOS Screen	122
Zoom the Current Window	123

Part Two
DESKTOP

Starting Desktop	126
Notepads	127

Outlines	141
Databases	142
Modem Telecommunications	152
Fax Telecommunications	156
Appointment Scheduler	158
Calculators	161
Macro Editor	162
Clipboard	163

Part Three
THE FILE AND DISK UTILITIES

PC Backup	166
Compress	169
PC Format	172
PC-Cache	174
Mirror	176
Rebuild	177
Diskfix	178
PC Secure	179

Appendix A
START-UP OPTIONS FOR SHELL AND DESKTOP
183

Appendix B
PC TOOLS PROGRAM FILES
185

Index — 189

Introduction

Quick! How do you format a new system disk using PC Tools Deluxe? Or how do you change the attributes of a subdirectory? Or how do you recover a file using the Delete Tracking method?

Unless you use PC Tools Deluxe heavily every day and use most or all of its features on a regular basis, sooner or later you'll come across a task that you won't remember how to do. It's only natural to forget procedures you don't repeat regularly. The solution: Look it up. There are three options for finding the information you need:

- Take a look at the the on-line help available in PC Tools Deluxe. The help is brief, though, and doesn't supply step-by-step instructions.

- Crack open the PC Tools Deluxe manual (actually, three manuals). Of course, that means you must wade through a lot of material just to find the steps you need to get the job done.

- Use this book, *PC Tools Deluxe 6 Instant Reference*, to find instructions quickly for using a command or function. You'll find compact and explicit directions for using all the major functions in PC Tools Deluxe, plus information on related topics. The organization of the topics helps you pinpoint them promptly and efficiently.

To adequately use this book, you should already be somewhat familiar with the basic functions of PC Tools Deluxe. If you are new to the program, I urge you to learn about it by reading the manuals that came with the software and by picking up a copy of *Mastering PC Tools Deluxe 6*, by Peter Dyson, SYBEX, 1990.

HOW THIS BOOK IS ORGANIZED

PC Tools Deluxe 6 Instant Reference is divided into three major parts:

- Part One covers the PC Shell program.
- Part Two covers the Desktop program.

- Part Three covers the assorted file and disk utility programs packaged with PC Tools, including PC Backup, PC Compress, PC Format, PC-Cache, Mirror, Rebuild, Diskfix, and PC Secure.

Part One comprises the majority of the book. In this section the topics are arranged alphabetically by command name; just flip through the pages until you find the command you want. Alternatively, you can look in the Table of Contents or Index, and turn to the indicated page.

In Part Two, each module of the Desktop program is detailed in a separate section. The topics within the sections are organized in approximately the same sequence as they appear in the pull-down menus. Only the more significant commands in the Desktop program are covered.

In Part Three, each utility program is described separately. Again, only the more significant commands of each program are covered.

This book covers both versions 5.5 and 6.0 of PC Tools. When the instructions for accessing a command are the same for both versions, the steps are combined in one entry. When the instructions differ—for example, when a command is invoked by pressing a different series of keys—the instructions for the two versions appear separately. Although this necessarily creates a certain amount of repetition, you'll be able to follow the sequence of steps for your version much more rapidly. There are also separate sequences of steps outlined for using the keyboard and using the mouse to access commands.

WHAT IS PC TOOLS DELUXE?

PC Tools is the best-selling utility program for the IBM PC and compatibles. It combines all the main features of DOS with sophisticated disk and file management tools. It offers four core functions:

- A *DOS shell*, for managing files and disks without the use of archaic DOS commands.
- *Data recovery*, for retrieving accidentally lost files and restructuring data on floppy and hard drives.

- *Hard-disk backup,* for making archival copies of your hard disk in case of data loss.
- *Desktop accessories,* including a word processor, data manager, and outliner, which you can use as stand-alone applications or as pop-up programs while using other software.

The Shell utility is the heart of PC Tools. It takes the place of DOS, providing all the basic functions available at the DOS prompt, such as copying files, formatting disks, and creating directories. But Shell makes working with your computer much easier, because it uses a convenient pull-down menu system for selecting commands. Want to format a 360K disk? Just pop the disk in the drive, and select the Format a Data Disk command. The options available while formatting disks are displayed along the way, so you don't have to remember DOS command-line switches.

Also central to PC Tools is its ability to recover data. The file Undelete command, available in the Shell program, can retrieve files you have accidentally erased. You can even recover subdirectories by using the Undelete command.

For sizable damage, you can use PC Tool's disk recovery programs: Diskfix, Mirror, and Rebuild. Diskfix, for example, analyzes the structure of your floppy and hard disks and looks for possible problems. Unlike a number of other disk recovery programs that are out now, Diskfix is entirely automatic. All you have to do is start the program and sit back as it attempts to repair your damaged disk. The Mirror and Rebuild programs take a snapshot of critical data on your hard disk in case this information is ever damaged.

The hard-drive backup program lets you archive the data on your hard drive to guard against possible data loss or damage. If something should happen to your hard drive, the backup files, placed on floppy disks or streaming tape, can be used to restore the lost information.

One of the great benefits of PC Tools is its user interface. With the exception of the Mirror, Rebuild, PC-Cache, and PC Format utilities, the programs in PC Tools follow the same display standards. Commands are located on pull-down menus, which you can access with the keyboard or mouse. Data is displayed in movable windows, and information is relayed to you in dialog and information boxes.

HARDWARE COMPATIBILITY

PC Tools works with the IBM PC, PC/XT, PC/AT, PS/2, and compatibles. PC Tools is not an alternative operating system, although it does supplement DOS. You need PC-DOS or MS-DOS version 3.0 or higher. I recommend that you use the latest version that works with your computer. To use PC Tools effectively, your computer should be outfitted with no less than 512K of RAM, preferably 640K. Expanded and extended RAM is not used unless you are running the PC-Cache disk-caching utility or are using Shell in memory-resident mode. PC Tools is designed explicitly for use with computers that have hard-disk drives.

USING A MOUSE

PC Tools is best used with a mouse. Commands can be selected using the keyboard, but you'll probably find that a mouse greatly enhances productivity. Throughout this book I outline the steps required to select a command with both the keyboard and the mouse.

PC Tools uses both buttons on a two-button mouse. If your mouse has three buttons, the center button is unused. The mouse functions vary somewhat, depending on the specific utility you are using. In general, the right button selects the current option. To use it, position the mouse pointer over the option you want to select, and push the right button. The right button is also used to scroll through file lists and through text. In the Shell program, the left button scrolls through a list of files and highlights (selects) them along the way.

There are four basic mouse functions used in PC Tools:

- *Moving* the mouse pointer entails nothing more than pushing the mouse on the table. The on-screen mouse pointer mimics your hand movements.

- *Clicking* selects on-screen items under the mouse pointer, such as options and menu commands. To click, hold the mouse still, and press the right button once.

- *Double-clicking* is the same as regular clicking except that you press the mouse button twice in quick succession. Generally, double-clicking is used to select an item on a list.
- *Dragging* is holding down the right or left mouse button while moving the mouse—for example, when copying a file from one subdirectory window to another. Release the mouse button when the selection is complete.

Part One

PC SHELL

PC Shell provides all the important DOS maintenance commands, enabling you to move, copy, delete, and compare disks, directories, and files in a window environment. The commands in this section are organized alphabetically for easy reference and include detailed steps for using the keyboard and the mouse in both version 5.5 and version 6.0.

ACTIVE LIST SWITCH

- **MENU**

  |6.0| Options➤Modify Display

  |5.5| Options

- **PURPOSE** Used with Two List Display, changes the currently active window between the first and second Tree/File List windows. Example: If the currently active window is the first Tree window, the command makes the second Tree window active. The active window is denoted by a double border. All other windows have a single border only.

To Switch the Currently Active List

Version 6.0

1. Press **Alt-O** to display the Options menu.
2. Press **O** to select the Modify Display command. The Modify Display submenu appears.
3. Press **A** to select the Active List Switch command.

1. Pull down the Options menu.
2. Select the Modify Display command. The Modify Display submenu appears.
3. Select the Active List Switch command.

Shortcuts When using the mouse, you can click within any window to make it the currently active window.

To toggle between the Tree and File List windows, press the **Tab** key.

Version 5.5

1. Press **Alt-O** to display the Options menu.
2. Press **A** to select the Active List Switch command.

1. Pull down the Options menu.
2. Select the Active List Switch command.

Shortcuts You can press the **F7** function key to choose the Active List Switch command.

When using the mouse, you can click within any window to make it the currently active window.

To toggle between the Tree and File List windows, press the **Tab** key.

See Also *Tree/Files Switch*. Swaps the active window between the Tree and File List windows.

ATTRIBUTE CHANGE

• MENU

File

4 ATTRIBUTE CHANGE

- **PURPOSE** Modifies the attributes or date and time of any currently selected file. The attributes are hidden, read-only, system, and archive.

  - *Time of creation or last edit.* Indicates the time of day the file was created or last edited in hours and minutes.

  - *Date of creation or last edit.* Indicates the date the file was created or last edited.

  - *Hidden.* Indicates whether the file is visible in a normal DOS directory (hidden OFF) or invisible (hidden ON). Shell displays all hidden files, regardless of the setting of this attribute.

  - *Read-only.* Indicates whether the file can be both read from and written to (read-only OFF) or just read from (read-only ON).

  - *System.* Indicates whether the file is reserved for system use (system ON) or regular application use (system OFF).

  - *Archive.* Indicates whether the file has recently been backed up (using any of several types of backup programs, including PC Tools Backup and DOS Backup). When archive is ON, the file is new or has been recently edited and is marked for backup. When archive is OFF, the file has already been backed up and can be skipped.

To Change the Attributes of a File

1. With the cursor keys, select one or more files in the File List window.
2. Press **Alt-F** to display the File menu.
3. Press **B** to choose the Attribute Change command. (Press **A** in version 5.5.) The Attribute Change dialog box appears.
4. To change the hidden, system, read-only, and archive attributes, type **H**, **S**, **R**, and **A**, respectively.

ATTRIBUTE CHANGE

5. To change the time, press → once and type the desired time. Follow the format *hh:mm*. Type **p** to indicate *p.m.* or **a** to indicate *a.m.* Example: **1:03p**.

6. To change the date, press → once more and type the desired date. Follow the format *mm/dd/yy*. Example: **08/08/91**.

When you are finished resetting the attributes and date and time for the file, do any one of the following:

- Press ↓ to select the next file in the list.
- Press **U** for **U**pdate to save the new attributes with the file.
- Press **X** for Exit to ignore changes to the file attributes.

1. Select one or more files in the File List window.

2. Pull down the File menu, and select the Attribute Change command. The Attribute Change dialog box appears.

3. To change the hidden, system, read-only, and archive attributes, type **H**, **S**, **R**, and **A**, respectively.

4. To change the time, click on the current time and type the new time. Follow the format *hh:mm*. Type **p** to indicate *p.m.* or **a** to indicate *a.m.* Example: **1:03p**.

5. To change the date, click on the current date and type the new date. Follow the format *mm/dd/yy*. Example: **08/08/91**.

When you are finished resetting the attributes and date and time for the file, do any one of the following:

- Click on the next file in the list.
- Click on the Update button to save the new attributes with the file.
- Click on the Exit button to ignore changes to the file attributes.

• NOTES The time and date are dependent on the system clock in your computer. The clock must be maintained (with a battery

6 BACKGROUND MAT

backup to keep it powered) or regularly updated each time the computer is turned on to display the correct time and date.

The archive attribute is automatically set when a file is created, edited, or backed up.

Under most circumstances, you should not change the system attribute of any file.

BACKGROUND MAT
Version 6.0 Only

- **MENU**

Options➤Setup Configuration

- **PURPOSE** Turns background pattern on or off.

To Turn Background Pattern On or Off

1. Press **Alt-O** to display the **O**ptions menu.
2. Press **C** to choose the Setup **C**onfiguration command. The Setup Configuration submenu appears. The current setting of the Background Mat is shown as ON or OFF.
3. Press **B** to choose the **B**ackground Mat command. The new setting of the command (either ON or OFF) is shown.
4. Press the **F3** function key to exit the menu.

1. Pull down the Options menu, and choose the Setup Configuration command. The Setup Configuration submenu

appears. The current setting of the Background Mat is shown as ON or OFF.

2. Click on the Background Mat command. The new setting of the command (either ON or OFF) is shown.

3. Click anywhere outside the menu to go back to Shell.

CHANGE DRIVE
Version 6.0 Only

● **MENU**

Disk

● **PURPOSE**   Changes the current drive and displays the directory tree and files for the active drive.

To Change to Another Drive

1. Press **Alt-D** to display the **D**isk menu.

2. Press **D** to choose the Change **D**rive command. A list appears displaying all valid drives.

3. Press the cursor keys to highlight the drive you want to change to.

4. Press ↵.

Shortcut   Press **Ctrl-***drive letter*, where the drive letter is **A**, **B**, **C**, or another valid drive. Example: To change to drive D, press **Ctrl-D**.

8 CHANGE USER LEVEL

1. Pull down the Disk menu, and select the Change Drive command. A list appears displaying all valid drives.
2. Double-click on the drive you want to change to.

Shortcut Click on one of the drive letters displayed above the Tree window.

CHANGE USER LEVEL
Version 6.0 Only

● **MENU**

Options➤Setup Configuration

● **PURPOSE** Changes the user level to beginning, intermediate, or advanced. Each user level has different commands on the pull-down menus.

To Change the User Level

1. Press **Alt-O** to display the **O**ptions menu.
2. Press **C** to choose the Setup **C**onfiguration command. The Setup Configuration submenu appears.
3. Press **U** to choose the Change **U**ser Level command. The Change User Level dialog box is displayed.
4. Press one of the following keys:
   - **B** to choose Beginner User Mode
   - **I** to choose Intermediate User Mode

- **A** to choose Advanced User Mode
5. You can optionally choose to have the Application menu pulled down each time Shell is started (press **L**).
6. Press ↵ to accept the changes, or press **C** to cancel.

1. Pull down the Options menu, and choose the Setup Configuration command. The Setup Configuration submenu appears.
2. Click on the Change User Level command. The Change User Level dialog box is displayed.
3. Click on one of the following:
   - Beginner User Mode
   - Intermediate User Mode
   - Advanced User Mode
4. You can optionally choose to have the Application menu pulled down each time Shell is started (click inside the check box).
5. Click on the OK button to accept the changes, or click on the Cancel button.

• **NOTES** Only the basic commands are provided at the beginning user level; all commands are available at the advanced user level. It is recommended that once you learn to use Shell, you leave the user level set to Advanced.

CLEAR FILE
Version 6.0 Only

• **MENU**

File

CLEAR FILE

- **PURPOSE** Erases a file from the disk and replaces the old data with null characters. You can use the Clear File command to make sure that the data from an old file cannot be accessed.

To Delete a File and Replace It with Null Characters

1. Press **Alt-F** to display the File menu.
2. Press **A** to choose the Clear File command. The Clear File dialog box appears.
3. Type the Replacement Hex Value character (default: F6), and press ↵ (or press ↵ alone to accept the default).
4. Type the number of overwrite cycles (default: 1), and press ↵ (or press ↵ alone to accept the default).
5. Type **Y** if you want to use U.S. Government security standards.
6. PC Tools warns you that the file cannot be undeleted. Verify that you want to clear the file by pressing **C** (for Clear), or press **X** for (Exit) to cancel the command.

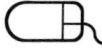

1. Pull down the File menu, and select the Clear File command. The Clear File dialog box appears. PC Tools warns you that the file cannot be undeleted.
2. Click on any of the option settings to change them, and type the new selections. At the last option, press ↵ to accept the new settings.
3. Verify that you want to clear the file by clicking on the Clear button, or click on the Exit button to cancel the command.

- **NOTES** Use the Clear File command with extreme caution. Once a file has been cleared, there is no way to retrieve it, even with the Shell Undelete command.

COMPARE

Version 5.5

See *Compare File*.

COMPARE DISK

- **MENU**

Disk

- **PURPOSE** Compares one disk with another. If the disks vary, even by one byte, Shell catches the discrepancy and indicates how the disks differ.

To Compare Two Disks

These steps apply whether you are using one or two drives for the disk comparison.

1. Press **Alt-D** to display the Disk menu.
2. Press **O** to choose the Compare Disk command.
3. Use the cursor keys to select a source drive, then press ↵.
4. Use the cursor keys to select a target drive, then press ↵.
5. Insert the source disk in the appropriate drive, and press ↵ to start the comparison.
6. Shell checks your command; press **C** (for Continue) to go on.

12 COMPARE DISK

7. When prompted by Shell, insert the target disk in the appropriate drive.

8. Press **C** (for **C**ompare or **C**ontinue as prompted) to complete the disk comparison.

These steps apply whether you are using one or two drives for the disk comparison.

1. Pull down the Disk menu, and choose the Compare Disk command.

2. Double-click on a drive letter to choose the source drive.

3. Click on a drive letter to choose the target drive.

4. Insert the source disk in the appropriate drive, and press ↵ to start the comparison.

5. Shell checks your command; click on the Continue button to go on.

6. When prompted by Shell, insert the target disk in the appropriate drive.

7. Click on the Continue button to complete the disk comparison.

• **NOTES** During the disk comparison, Shell displays a progress indicator. The program displays the status of each track on the disk as it does the comparison:

R   Reading the track
C   Comparing the track
. (dot) Track compared successfully

You can compare disks using two drives *only* if the drives are the same size and capacity. For example, you can compare disks in two 5¼-inch 360K drives, but not in a 5¼-inch and a 3½-inch drive.

If you have one drive, Shell may ask you to swap the target and source disks in the drive several times to complete the comparison.

COMPARE FILE

• MENU

File

• PURPOSE
Compares the contents of two files and determines whether they are identical. The command can also compare several sets of files at the same time, or one file with a number of other files. The following steps assume one file is being compared with another.

To Compare Two Files

This procedure applies only if you are using One List Display.

1. With the cursor keys, select one of the files you want to compare.
2. Press **Alt-F** to display the File menu.
3. Press **O** to choose the Compare File command.
4. With the cursor keys, indicate the drive that contains the file you want to compare with, and press ↵.
5. Press **M** (for Matching Names) or **D** (for Different Names), depending on whether the two files share the same name.
6. With the cursor keys, indicate the directory that contains the file you want to compare with, and press ↵.
7. Type the name of the second file in the File Compare dialog box, and press ↵.
8. Press **C** for Continue to compare the files, or press **X** for Exit to cancel the file comparison.

Shell now compares the file, checking to make sure it is the same size. Differences, if any, are noted.

14 COPY DISK

1. Select one of the files you want to compare.
2. Pull down the File menu, and choose the Compare File command.
3. Double-click on the drive letter that contains the file you want to compare with.
4. Click on the Matching Names button or Different Names button, depending on whether the two files share the same name.
5. Click on the directory that contains the file you want to compare with.
6. Type the name of the second file in the File Compare dialog box, and click on the Compare button (or press ↵).
7. Click on the Continue button to complete the file comparison, or click on the Exit button to cancel.

Shell now compares the file, checking to make sure it is the same size. Differences, if any, are noted.

COPY
Version 5.5

See *Copy File*.

COPY DISK

• MENU

Disk

COPY DISK

- **PURPOSE** Creates a duplicate image of a floppy on another disk. The copy includes all files (hidden, system, or otherwise), as well as all subdirectories and their contents. The Copy Disk command can be used for single- or dual-drive copies. To make dual-drive copies, both drives must be the same size and have the same format capacity.

To Make a Copy of a Floppy Disk

1. Press **Alt-D** to display the Disk menu.
2. Press **C** to choose the Copy Disk command.
3. Use the cursor keys to select a source drive (the drive that holds the original disk), then press ↵.
4. Use the cursor keys to select a target drive (the drive that will hold the copy), then press ↵.
5. Insert the source disk in the appropriate drive, and press ↵ to start copying.
6. Shell checks your command; press **C** to go on.
7. When prompted by Shell, insert the target disk in the appropriate drive.
8. Press **C** to complete the copying of the disk.

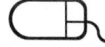

1. Pull down the Disk menu, and choose the Copy Disk command.
2. Double-click on a drive letter to choose the source drive (the drive that will hold the original disk).
3. Click on a drive letter to choose the target drive (the drive that will hold the copy).
4. Insert the source disk in the appropriate drive, and press ↵ to start copying.

16 COPY FILE

5. Shell checks your command; click on the Copy button (version 6.0) or the Continue button (version 5.5) to go on.

6. When prompted by Shell, insert the target disk in the appropriate drive.

7. Click on the Copy button (version 6.0) or the Continue button (version 5.5) to complete the copying of the disk.

COPY FILE

- **MENU**

File

- **PURPOSE** Copies files from one disk or directory to another.

To Copy a File

1. Select the disk and directory that holds the file you want to copy.

2. Use the cursor keys to highlight the file in the File List window.

3. Press **Alt-F** to display the File menu.

4. Press **C** to choose the Copy File command.

5. Use the cursor keys to select the drive where you want to copy the file. Press ↵.

6. Use the cursor keys to select a subdirectory for the copied file, if any.

7. In the File Copy dialog box, type a name for the copied file. Shell initially provides the same name as the original.

COPY FILE 17

If you are copying to a different disk or directory, you can keep the old name.

8. Press ↵ to accept the new name.

9. Verify the copy command, and press ↵ to complete the copying of the file.

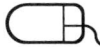

1. Select the disk and directory that holds the file you want to copy.

2. Click on the file in the File List window.

3. Pull down the File menu, and choose the Copy File command.

4. Click on the drive where you want to copy the file.

5. Select a subdirectory for the copied file, if any.

6. In the File Copy dialog box, type a name for the copied file. Shell initially provides the same name as the original. If you are copying to a different disk or directory, you can keep the old name.

7. Click on the OK button to accept the new name.

8. Verify the copy command, and click on the OK button to complete the copying of the file.

Shortcut If you are using a mouse, you can "drag copy" files. The procedure works best in Two List Display.

1. In one list, select the disk and directory that contains the file you want to copy.

2. In the other list, select the disk and directory where you want to copy the file.

3. Click on the file you want to copy.

4. While holding down the left mouse button, drag the mouse pointer into the destination File List window.

5. Release the mouse button.

As you drag the mouse with the file in tow, Shell indicates that you are copying one or more files. This technique works only when copying files from one disk or directory to another. The names of the original files are kept.

- **NOTES** You can copy more than one file at a time, using any of the three methods outlined above. Select all the files you want to copy, then follow the same steps you use to copy a single file. When using the Copy File command (with the keyboard or mouse), Shell asks you to provide a new name for each file in the group. You are not prompted for new file names when using the mouse drag-copy shortcut technique.

See Also *Move File*. Moves files between directories and disks.

DATE/TIME

- **MENU**

    6.0 Options➤Setup Configuration

    5.5 Options

- **PURPOSE** Sets the time and date on the clock used by DOS and applications. The Date/Time command serves the same purpose as the TIME and DATE commands in DOS.

To Change the Clock's Date and Time

Version 6.0

1. Press **Alt-O** to display the **O**ptions menu.

DATE/TIME 19

2. Press **C** to choose the Setup Configuration command. The Setup Configuration submenu appears.

3. Press **T** to choose the Date/Time command. The Date/Time dialog box appears.

4. Type the new date, following the format *mm/dd/yy*, and press ↵. Example: **06/10/91**.

5. Type the new time, following the format *hh/mm*, and press ↵. Use 24-hour time. Example: **17:06** (5:06 p.m.).

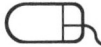

1. Pull down the Options menu, and choose the Setup Configuration command. The Setup Configuration submenu appears.

2. Choose the Date/Time command from the submenu. The Date/Time dialog box appears.

3. Type the new date, following the format *mm/dd/yy*, and press ↵. Example: **06/10/91**.

4. Type the new time, following the format *hh/mm*, and press ↵. Use 24-hour time. Example: **17:06** (5:06 p.m.).

Version 5.5

1. Press **Alt-O** to display the Options menu.

2. Press **E** to choose the Date/Time command. The Date/Time dialog box appears.

3. Type the new date, following the format *mm/dd/yy*, and press ↵. Example: **06/10/91**.

4. Type the new time, following the format *hh/mm*, and press ↵. Use 24-hour time. Example: **17:06** (5:06 p.m.).

DEFAULT VIEWER

1. Pull down the Options menu, and choose the Date/Time command. The Date/Time dialog box appears.
2. Type the new date, following the format *mm/dd/yy*, and press ↵. Example: **06/10/91**.
3. Type the new time, following the format *hh/mm*, and press ↵. Use 24-hour time. Example: **17:06** (5:06 p.m.).

DEFAULT VIEWER
Version 6.0 Only

- **MENU**

Options➤Setup Configuration

- **PURPOSE** Changes the way files are displayed when viewed (except document files created by applications supported by Shell, such as dBASE III and WordStar). You have your choice of initially displaying the file in either ASCII or binary hexadecimal format.

To Change the Displayed View of Files

1. Press **Alt-O** to display the Options menu.
2. Press **C** to choose the Setup Configuration command. The Setup Configuration submenu appears. The current setting of the Default Viewer command is shown as TEXT (for ASCII display) or BINARY (for hexadecimal display).
3. Press **D** to choose the Default Viewer command. The new setting of the command (either TEXT or BINARY) is shown.

DEFINE FUNCTION KEYS   21

4. Press the **F3** function key to exit the menu.

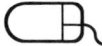

1. Pull down the Options menu, and choose the Setup Configuration command. The Setup Configuration submenu appears. The current setting of the Default Viewer command is shown as TEXT (for ASCII display) or BINARY (for hexadecimal display).

2. Click on the Default Viewer command. The new setting of the command (either TEXT or BINARY) is shown.

3. Click anywhere outside the menu to go back to Shell.

DEFINE FUNCTION KEYS
Version 6.0 Only

- **MENU**

Options➤Setup Configuration

- **PURPOSE** Changes the action of the function keys. The definitions of the new functions are displayed at the bottom of the Shell screen. Three of the function keys (F1, F3, and F10) cannot be changed.

To Change the Action of the Function Keys

1. Press **Alt-O** to display the Options menu.
2. Press **C** to choose the Setup Configuration command. The Setup Configuration submenu appears.

22 DEFINE FUNCTION KEYS

3. Press **F** to choose the Define Function Keys command. The Define Function Keys dialog box appears.

4. Use the cursor keys to highlight a function key you want to change (F1, F3, and F10 are not changeable).

5. Press the **Tab** key to activate the Available Functions window.

6. Use the cursor keys to highlight a new command.

7. Press ↵ to assign the new command to the selected function key. You may repeat the process for the remaining function keys, as desired.

8. Press the function key **F3** when you're finished.

9. When prompted, press **S** to save the new function keys, or press **C** to cancel.

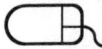

1. Pull down the Options menu, and choose the Setup Configuration command. The Setup Configuration submenu appears.

2. Click on the Define Function Keys command. The Define Function Keys dialog box appears.

3. Click on a function key you want to change (F1, F3, and F10 are not changeable).

4. Click inside the Available Functions window to activate it.

5. Scroll through the list and highlight a new command.

6. Click on a command; it will be assigned to the selected function key. You may repeat the process for the remaining function keys, as desired.

7. Click inside the Close box in the upper-left corner of the Define Function Keys dialog box when you're finished.

8. When prompted, click on Save to keep the new function keys, or click on Cancel to quit.

- **NOTES** The following are the functions Shell initially provides for the function keys. The shortcut menu name is used at the bottom of the Shell display to indicate the current function of each key. Those keys that are listed as *not changeable* cannot be redefined.

Key	Function	Menu Name
F1	not changeable	Help
F2	Quick File View	Qview
F3	not changeable	Exit
F4	Unselect Files	Unsel
F5	Copy File	Copy
F6	File Display Options	Disply
F7	Locate File	Locate
F8	Zoom Current Window	Zoom
F9	File Select Filter	Select
F10	not changeable	Menu

The new definitions for the function keys are kept in the PCSHELL.CFG file. If this file is erased or damaged, the definitions will be lost.

DELETE
Version 5.5

See *Delete File*.

DELETE FILE

● MENU

File

24 DELETE FILE

● **PURPOSE**   Erases one or more selected files from the disk. The Delete File command can be used with all files, regardless of their attributes; you can readily erase files with read-only, hidden, and system attributes.

To Delete a File

[KEY]

1. Use the cursor keys to highlight the file you want to delete.
2. Press **Alt-F** to display the File command.
3. Press **D** to choose the Delete File command.
4. Verify that you want to erase the file by pressing **D** (for Delete), or press **C** (for Cancel) to terminate the command.

Shortcut   You can delete several files at the same time by highlighting each one in turn and pressing ↵ to select it. Shell numbers each file as you select it so that you know how many files you are about to delete.

1. Click on the file you want to delete.
2. Pull down the File menu, and choose the Delete File command.
3. Verify that you want to erase the file by clicking on the Delete button, or click on the Cancel button to terminate the command.

Shortcut   You can delete several files at the same time by clicking on each one, then choosing the Delete File command. You can also use the "drag select" method of selecting multiple files.

See Also   *Undelete File.* Reclaims files that you have accidentally erased.

DIRECTORY MAINT

● **MENU**

Disk

● **PURPOSE** Provides a suite of commands for maintaining disk subdirectories. Using the Directory Maintenance commands, you can do the following:

- Add a new subdirectory.
- Create a subdirectory.
- Delete a subdirectory.
- Change the currently logged subdirectory to a new one (available in version 5.5 only).
- Prune and graft a subdirectory to move it (and the files it contains) into another directory.
- Modify certain attributes of a directory, including *hidden* (hides the directory when you use the DIR command in DOS), *system* (marks the subdirectory for system use), *archive* (marks the subdirectory for archiving during the next backup), and *read-only* (prevents the subdirectory from being deleted).

To Add a New Subdirectory

[KEY]

1. Press **Alt-D** to display the **D**isk menu.
2. Press **M** to choose the Directory **M**aintenance command. The Directory Maintenance submenu appears.
3. Press **A** to choose the **A**dd a Subdirectory command.
4. Use the cursor keys in the Tree window to indicate where you want to add the new subdirectory. **Note:** If you're

26 DIRECTORY MAINT

working with a disk that doesn't have subdirectories, like a floppy disk, Shell won't prompt you to select a location for adding the new subdirectory.

5. Press C for Continue.

6. Type a name for the subdirectory (up to eight characters and an optional three-character extension). Press ↵ or **Alt-C** when you're finished.

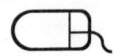

1. Pull down the Disk menu, and choose the Directory Maintenance command. The Directory Maintenance submenu appears.

2. Choose the Add a Subdirectory command.

3. In the Tree window, double-click on the location where you want to add the new subdirectory. **Note:** If you're working with a disk that doesn't have subdirectories, like a floppy disk, Shell won't prompt you to select a location for adding the new subdirectory.

4. Type a name for the subdirectory (up to eight characters and an optional three-character extension).

5. Click on the Continue button when you're finished.

To Rename a Subdirectory

1. Press **Alt-D** to display the Disk menu.

2. Press **M** to choose the Directory **M**aintenance command. The Directory Maintenance submenu appears.

3. Press **R** to choose the **R**ename a Subdirectory command.

4. Use the cursor keys in the Tree window to select a subdirectory to rename.

5. Press C for Continue.

DIRECTORY MAINT 27

6. Type a new name for the subdirectory (up to eight characters and an optional three-character extension). Press ↵ or **Alt-C** when you're finished.

🖱

1. Pull down the Disk menu, and choose the Directory Maintenance command. The Directory Maintenance submenu appears.
2. Choose the Rename a Subdirectory command.
3. In the Tree window, double-click on the subdirectory you want to rename.
4. Type a new name for the subdirectory (up to eight characters and an optional three-character extension).
5. Click on the Continue button when you're finished.

To Delete a Subdirectory

[KEY]

1. Press **Alt-D** to display the **D**isk menu.
2. Press **M** to choose the Directory **M**aintenance command. The Directory Maintenance submenu appears.
3. Press **D** to choose the **D**elete a Subdirectory command.
4. Use the cursor keys in the Tree window to select a subdirectory to erase.
5. Press **C** for **C**ontinue.
6. Confirm the deletion by again pressing **C** for **C**ontinue.

🖱

1. Pull Down the Disk menu, and choose the Directory Maintenance command. The Directory Maintenance submenu appears.

28 DIRECTORY MAINT

2. Choose the Delete a Subdirectory command.
3. In the Tree window, double-click on the subdirectory you want to delete.
4. Click on the Continue button to confirm the deletion.

• **NOTES**   You cannot delete a subdirectory if it is not empty, or if it is the current DOS directory (in 5.5 signified by a check mark beside the directory name).

To Change the Logged Drive to Another Directory—Version 5.5 Only

[KEY]

1. Press **Alt-D** to display the **D**isk menu.
2. Press **M** to choose the Directory **M**aintenance command. The Directory Maintenance submenu appears.
3. Press **C** to choose the **C**hange DOS Current command.
4. Use the cursor keys in the Tree window to choose the subdirectory you want to make current.
5. Press **C** for **C**ontinue.

1. Pull down the Disk menu, and choose the Directory Maintenance command. The Directory Maintenance submenu appears.
2. Choose the Change DOS Current command.
3. In the Tree window, double-click on the subdirectory you want to make current.

DIRECTORY MAINT   29

To Prune and Graft a Subdirectory

KEY

1. Press **Alt-D** to display the **D**isk menu.
2. Press **M** to choose the Directory **M**aintenance command. The Directory Maintenance submenu appears.
3. Press **P** to choose the **P**rune and Graft command.
4. Use the cursor keys in the Tree window to select a subdirectory to take items from (this is *pruning*).
5. Press **C** for **C**ontinue twice. The directory to prune is shown with a > symbol.
6. Use the cursor keys in the Tree window to select a subdirectory to add the items to (this is *grafting*).
7. Press **C** for **C**ontinue.
8. Press **C** (for **C**ontinue) to confirm the prune-and-graft operation, or press **X** (for E**x**it) to cancel the operation.

1. Pull down the Disk menu, and choose the Directory Maintenance command. The Directory Maintenance submenu appears.
2. Choose the Prune and Graft command.
3. In the Tree window, double-click on the subdirectory you want to take items from (this is *pruning*). The directory to prune is shown with a > symbol.
4. In the Tree window, double-click on the subdirectory to add the items to (this is *grafting*).
5. Click on the Continue button to confirm the prune-and-graft operation, or click on the Exit button to cancel the operation.

30 DIRECTORY MAINT

To Modify Subdirectory Attributes

[KEY]

1. Press **Alt-D** to display the Disk menu.
2. Press **M** to choose the Directory **M**aintenance command. The Directory Maintenance submenu appears.
3. Press **M** to choose the **M**odify Attributes command.
4. Use the cursor keys in the Tree window to select a subdirectory to modify.
5. Press **C** for **C**ontinue. The Modify Directory Attributes dialog box appears.
6. Press **H**, **S**, **R**, and **A** to change the hidden, system, read-only, and archive attributes, respectively.
7. Press **U** (for **U**pdate) to accept the new attributes, or press **C** (for **C**ancel) to end the operation.

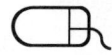

1. Pull down the Disk menu, and choose the Directory Maintenance command. The Directory Maintenance submenu appears.
2. Choose the Modify Attributes command.
3. In the Tree window, double-click on the subdirectory you want to modify. The Modify Directory Attributes submenu appears.
4. Press **H**, **S**, **R**, and **A** to change the hidden, system, read-only, and archive attributes, respectively.
5. Click on the Update button to accept the new attributes, or click on the Cancel button to cancel the command.

• **NOTES** When working with directories, Shell may not immediately display your changes. You can force the program to recognize the new directory structure by choosing the Re-Read the Tree command on the Options menu.

DIRECTORY SORT

● **MENU**

Special

● **PURPOSE**   Organizes the files in a selected directory or on a selected disk in alphabetical or numerical order. You can select ascending (A to Z) or descending (Z to A) order and can make the sort temporary or permanent.

To Sort a Directory

[KEY]

1. Select the drive and/or directory you want to sort (press the **Ctrl** key and a drive letter, such as **Ctrl-D**).
2. Press **Alt-S** to display the Special menu.
3. Press **D** to choose the Directory Sort command.
4. Press **1** through **5** to indicate the sort key:

    1 Sort by name
    2 Sort by extension
    3 Sort by size
    4 Sort by date/time
    5 Sort by select number (sorts files in the order you previously selected them in the File List window)

5. Press **6** if you want to sort in ascending order, or press **7** if you want to sort in descending order.
6. Press **S** (for **S**ort) or **C** (for **C**ancel).
7. In the Directory Sort dialog box, indicate how you want the sort displayed. Select **V**iew to see the sort in Shell only, select **U**pdate to change the disk directory itself, or select

Resort to choose new sorting parameters. Press **V**, **U**, or **R**, as desired (or **C** for **C**ancel).

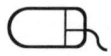

1. Click on the drive and/or directory you want to sort.
2. Pull down the Special menu, and choose the Directory Sort command.
3. Click on one of the key options:
   Sort by name
   Sort by extension
   Sort by size
   Sort by date/time
   Sort by select number (sorts files in the order you previously selected them in the File List window)
4. Click on Ascending or Descending, as desired, then click on the Sort button.
5. In the Directory Sort dialog box, indicate how you want the sort displayed. You can click on View to see the sort in Shell only, click on Update to change the disk directory itself, or click on Resort to choose new sorting parameters. Click on Cancel to quit.

• **NOTES**   The Directory Sort command is generally used to permanently sort the files on a disk or in a directory. If you merely want to view files in alphabetical order from within Shell, use the File Display Options command to turn File List sorting on and off.

DISK INFO

• **MENU**

Disk

DISK INFO

- **PURPOSE** Displays capacity and formatting information about the currently active disk. This information includes the following:

  - Total disk space, in bytes
  - Available space, in bytes
  - Space allocated to hidden files, in bytes
  - Space allocated to user files, in bytes
  - Space allocated to directories, in bytes
  - Space allocated to bad sectors, in bytes
  - Number of bytes per sector
  - Number of sectors per cluster
  - Number of sectors per track
  - Total number of clusters for the entire disk
  - Total number of sectors for the entire disk
  - Total number of tracks for the entire disk
  - Number of disk sides (usually more than two for hard disks)
  - Number of track cylinders

To Display Information about a Disk

KEY

1. Select a drive to check (press **Ctrl** and the letter of the drive).
2. Press **Alt-D** to display the Disk menu.
3. Press **I** to choose the Disk Info command. The Disk Information box appears.
4. Press **X** for Exit to leave the box.

34 DISK MAP

1. Select a drive to check (click on a drive letter above the Tree window).
2. Pull down the Disk menu, and choose the Disk Info command. The Disk Information box appears.
3. Click on the Exit button to leave the box.

See Also *System Info, Disk Map, File Map, Memory Map.* These commands display additional information about your disks and computer.

DISK MAP

● **MENU**

Special

● **PURPOSE** Displays a "bird's-eye view" of the used and unused portions of your disks, showing sectors that are used for the boot record, file allocation table (FAT), directory, hidden files, read-only files, bad clusters, and allocated (user) files. Also displays available (free) space.

To See Which Sectors Are Used by Which Files

1. Select a drive to check (press **Ctrl** and the letter of the drive).
2. Press **Alt-S** to display the **S**pecial menu.
3. Press **M** to choose the Disk **M**ap command. The Disk Mapping information box appears.

4. Press **X** for Exit to leave the box.

1. Select a drive to check (click on a drive letter above the Tree window).
2. Pull down the Special menu, and choose the Disk Map command. The Disk Mapping information box appears.
3. Click on the Exit button to leave the box.

● **NOTES** The Disk Mapping information box uses symbols to designate how space is used on the disk.

Symbol	Meaning
Shade	Space available
. (dot)	Space allocated to user files
B	Boot record
F	File allocation table (FAT)
D	Directory
h	Hidden file
r	Read-only file
x	Bad sector (as marked in the file allocation table when the disk was formatted)

On very large drives (hard drives over 20 or 30 megabytes), the boot record, file allocation table, and directory sectors are not shown.

See Also *System Info, File Map, Disk Info, Memory Map.* These commands display additional information about your disks and computer.

DOS COMMAND LINE
Version 6.0 Only

• MENU

Options➤Setup Configuration

• **PURPOSE** Turns the DOS command line that appears near the bottom of the Shell display on or off. When it's turned on, you can directly enter a DOS command while in Shell. **Note:** You must also have Short Cut Keys set to OFF (also set with the Setup Configuration command).

To Turn DOS Command Line On or Off

KEY

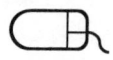

1. Press **Alt-O** to display the **O**ptions menu.
2. Press **C** to choose the Setup **C**onfiguration command. The Setup Configuration submenu appears. The current setting of DOS Command Line is shown as ON or OFF.
3. Press **C** to choose the DOS **C**ommand Line command. The new setting of the command (either ON or OFF) is shown.
4. Press the **F3** function key to exit the menu.

1. Pull down the Options menu, and choose the Setup Configuration command. The Setup Configuration submenu appears. The current setting of DOS Command Line is shown as ON or OFF.
2. Click on the DOS Command Line command. The new setting of the command (either ON or OFF) is shown.
3. Click anywhere outside the menu to return to Shell.

- **NOTES**   To enter a command, simply begin typing. If you press ↵, Shell will temporarily exit you to DOS, where your command will be executed. After the command is finished, press any key to reenter Shell. Shell automatically restarts if you have the Wait on DOS Screen option (on the Setup Configuration menu) set to OFF).

See Also   *Short Cut Keys.* Turns the shortcut command menu on and off. It must be set to OFF to view the DOS command line. Use the *Wait on DOS Screen* command to wait after executing a command before returning to Shell.

EDIT FILE

- **MENU**

File

- **PURPOSE**   Creates and edits any file. The Edit File (or File Edit in version 5.5) command is most often used to edit or view text-only or ASCII files.

To Edit a File

[KEY]

1. Use the cursor keys to select the file you want to edit (when creating a new file, select any existing file).
2. Press **Alt-F** to display the File menu.
3. Press **E** to choose the Edit File command.
4. Press **E** to edit the selected file, or press **C** to create a new file.
5. Make changes to the file as desired.
6. Save the document when you're finished by pressing Alt-S, then press **C** for Continue.

7. Press **F3** to return to Shell. (Alternatively, for steps 6 and 7, you can press **Esc** and then press **S** for **S**ave.)

1. Click on the file you want to edit (to create a new file, select any existing file).
2. Pull down the File menu, and choose the Edit File command.
3. Click on the Edit button to edit the selected file, or click on the Create button to create a new file.
4. Make changes to the file as desired.
5. Save the document when you're finished by pressing Alt-S, then click on the Continue button.
6. Click in the Close box of the Edit window to return to Shell.

• **NOTES** The Shell file editor works like most computer word processors and is generally self-explanatory. You press a key to enter a character at the cursor, press ↵ to start a new line, and so forth. You can use the Delete and Backspace keys to remove characters you don't want. If you want to overwrite existing characters, press the Insert key (the INS indicator disappears). This puts you in Typeover mode. Press Insert again to return to Insert mode.

The file editor also includes rudimentary word processing features. You can access these features by pressing the Alt key in combination with a letter key. The available commands are displayed along the bottom of the screen.

Table 1.1 lists the editing keys you can use in the file editor.

See Also *Hex Edit, Notepads* (in Desktop utility). You can use the hex editor to edit binary files, such as program files or documents created by applications. You can use the Notepads utility as a word processor for creating or editing files formatted for ASCII and WordStar.

Table 1.1: File Editor Editing Keys

FUNCTION	KEY
Enter hard return	↵
Enter tab	Tab
Delete character under cursor	Delete
Delete character to left of cursor	Backspace
Move down one line	↓
Move up one line	↑
Move right one character	→
Move left one character	←
Move to start of line	Home
Move to end of line	End
Move to start of file	Ctrl-Home
Move to end of file	Ctrl-End
Move to top of window	Home, Home
Move to bottom of window	End, End
Move up one window	PgUp
Move down one window	PgDn

EXIT PC SHELL

- **MENU**

File

- **PURPOSE**   Exits you from the Shell program and returns you to DOS.

To Leave Shell and Return to DOS

[KEY]

1. Press **Alt-F** to display the File menu.
2. Press **X** to choose the Exit PC Shell command.
3. Verify that you want to exit by pressing **X**, or press **C** for Continue to remain in PC Shell.

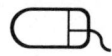

1. Pull down the File menu, and choose the Exit PC Shell command.
2. Click on the Exit button to leave PC Shell, or click on the Continue button to remain in Shell.

Shortcut Press the function key **F3**, then **X** for Exit.

- **NOTES** When using version 6.0, Shell displays a third option when exiting the program if you have modified any of the file or window display parameters. Press **S** (or click on the Save button) to save any changes, or press **X** for Exit to forfeit any changes you have made during the current session.

FILE DISPLAY OPTIONS

- **MENU**

  6.0 Options➤Modify Display

  5.5 Options

FILE DISPLAY OPTIONS

- **PURPOSE** Sets the information displayed and how the files are sorted in the File List window. For all files displayed, you can choose to include the size, date, time, attribute (such as read-only or hidden), and number of clusters the file occupies on the disk. You can sort using any of the following as a sort key:

  - File name
  - File-name extension
  - File size
  - Date/time

You can further define an ascending or a descending sort, or turn sorting off.

To Set How Files Are Displayed and Sorted

Version 6.0

[KEY]

1. Press **Alt-O** to display the Options menu.
2. Press **O** to select the Modify Display command. The Modify Display submenu appears.
3. Press **D** to select the File Display Options command. The Display Options dialog box appears.
4. Press one or more of the following number keys to set the information displayed with all files:

   0 Size
   1 Date
   2 Time
   3 Attribute
   4 Number of clusters

5. Press any one of the following number keys to set the sort order (or press **B** if you don't want the files sorted):

   5 Name
   6 Extension

42 FILE DISPLAY OPTIONS

    7   Size
    8   Date/Time

6. Press **9** for ascending sort, or press **A** for descending sort.

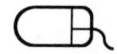

7. Press ↵ when you're finished.

1. Pull down the Options menu, and choose the Modify Display command. The Modify Display submenu appears.

2. Choose the File Display Options command. The Display Options dialog box appears.

3. Click on one of the display options (numbers 0 through 4) to set the information displayed with each file.

4. Click on one of the file sort options (numbers 5 through 8) to set the sort order, or click on No Sort to turn sorting off.

5. Click on Ascending or Descending as desired.

6. Click on the OK button when you're finished.

Shortcut   Press the function key **F6** to immediately access the Display Options dialog box.

Version 5.5

1. Press **Alt-O** to display the Options menu.

2. Press **I** to select the File Display Options command. The Set File Display Options dialog box appears.

3. Press one or more of the following number keys to set the information displayed with all files:

    0   Size
    1   Date
    2   Time

FILE DISPLAY OPTIONS 43

     3 Attribute

     4 Number of clusters

4. Press any one of the following number keys to set the sort order (or press **B** if you don't want the files sorted):

     5 Name

     6 Extension

     7 Size

     8 Date/Time

5. Press **9** for ascending sort, or press **A** for descending sort.

6. Press ↵ when you're finished.

1. Pull down the Options menu, and choose the File Display Options command. The Set File Display Options dialog box appears.

2. Click on any of the display options (numbers 0 through 4) to set the information displayed with each file.

3. Click on one of the file sort options (numbers 5 through 8) to set the sort order, or click on No Sort to turn sorting off.

4. Click on Ascending or Descending as desired.

5. Click on the OK button when you're finished.

Shortcut   Press the function key **F6** to immediately access the Set File Display Options dialog box.

See Also   *File List Filter, File Select Filter.* The File List Filter command limits the files displayed in the File List window, based on the name parameters you supply. The File Select Filter command automatically selects only those files that match the name parameters you supply.

FILE EDIT
Version 5.5

See *Edit File*.

FILE LIST FILTER

- **MENU**

    6.0 Options➤Modify Display

    5.5 Options

- **PURPOSE** Limits the files displayed in the File List window, according to file-name parameters you supply. You can use wildcards (* and ?) to display files with common names and extensions. The default is *.*, which displays all files.

To Change the Display Parameters for the File List Window

Version 6.0

KEY

1. Press **Alt-O** to display the Options menu.
2. Press **O** to choose the Modify Display command. The Modify Display submenu appears.
3. Press **L** to choose the File List Filter command. The File List Filter dialog box appears.

FILE LIST FILTER 45

4. Type the list parameters, using wildcards as desired. Press the **Tab** key to move from the Name field to the Extension field. Example: To list only batch files, enter * in the Name field and **BAT** in the Extension field. Press the **Tab** key again.

5. Press **S** (for **S**elect) to accept the new list parameters. (Pressing **Alt-S** replaces the last two actions.)

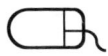

1. Pull down the Options menu, and choose the Modify Display command. The Modify Display submenu appears.

2. Choose the File List Filter command. The File List Filter dialog box appears.

3. Type the list parameters, using wildcards as desired. Press the **Tab** key to move from the Name field to the Extension field. Example: To list only batch files, enter * in the Name field and **BAT** in the Extension field.

4. Click on the Select button to accept the new list parameters.

Shortcut   Press **R** (for **R**eset) to display all files in the File List window. The Reset button serves the same purpose as typing *.* in the Name and Extension fields within the File List Filter dialog box.

Version 5.5

1. Press **Alt-O** to display the Options menu.

2. Press **L** to choose the File List Filter command. The File List Filter dialog box appears.

3. Type the list parameters, using wildcards as desired. Press the **Tab** key to move from the Name field to the Extension field. Example: To list only batch files, enter * in the Name field and **BAT** in the Extension field. Press the **Tab** key again.

FILE LIST WINDOW

4. Press **S** (for **S**elect) to accept the new list parameters. (Pressing **Alt-S** replaces these last two actions.)

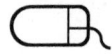

1. Pull down the Options menu, and choose the File List Filter command. The File List Filter dialog box appears.

2. Type the list parameters, using wildcards as desired. Press the **Tab** key to move from the Name field to the Extension field. Example: To list only batch files, enter * in the Name field and **BAT** in the Extension field.

3. Click on the Select button to accept the new list parameters.

Shortcuts   Press **R** (for **R**eset) to display all files in the File List window. The Reset button serves the same purpose as typing *.* in the Name and Extension fields within the File List Filter dialog box.

If you are using the keyboard, press the function key **F8** to immediately access the File List Filter dialog box.

See Also   *File Display Options, File Select Filter.* The File Display Options command sets the information displayed for each file, as well as how the files are sorted in the File List window. The File Select Filter command selects only those files that meet the file-name parameters you supply.

FILE LIST WINDOW
Version 6.0 Only

● **MENU**

Options

- **PURPOSE** Turns the File List window on and off. The current setting of the File List window is shown next to the command in the pull-down menu. The command acts as a toggle: Choose it once to turn off the File List window; choose it again to turn the window back on.

To Turn the File List Window On and Off

[KEY]

1. Press **Alt-O** to display the Options menu.
2. Press **F** to choose the File List Window command.

🖱

1. Pull down the Options menu.
2. Choose the File List Window command.

FILE MAP

- **MENU**

Special

- **PURPOSE** Visually displays the relative location on the disk of a selected file. The File Map command allows you to easily spot large files or files that are fragmented throughout several noncontiguous sectors on the disk.

To Display the Clusters Allocated to Specific Files

[KEY]

1. In the File List window, use the cursor keys to select a file to view.
2. Press **Alt-S** to display the Special menu.
3. Press **F** to choose the File Map command. The File Mapping information box appears. Clusters allocated to the selected file are indicated by a dotted rectangle.
4. Press **Esc** to close the information box.

1. In the File List window, click on a file to view.
2. Pull down the Special menu, and choose the File Map command. The File Mapping information box appears. Clusters allocated to the selected file are indicated by a dotted rectangle.
3. Click on the Cancel button to close the information box.

• **NOTES** While in the File Mapping information box, press N (or click on the Next button) to view the next file in the File List window. Press P (or click on the Prior button) to view the previous file.

The File Mapping information box uses symbols to show how disk space is used:

Shade	Space available
. (dot)	Space allocated to user files
B	Boot record
F	File allocation table
D	Directory
h	Hidden file

r   Read-only file

x   Bad sector (as marked in the file allocation table when the disk was formatted)

On very large drives (hard drives over 20 or 30 megabytes), the boot record, file allocation table, and directory sectors are not shown.

See Also   *Disk Map.* Displays the allocation of space for all files on the disk.

FILE SELECT FILTER

• MENU

|6.0| Options➤Modify Display

|5.5| Options

• **PURPOSE**   Selects only those files in the File List window that meet the file-name parameters you supply. You can use wildcards (* and ?) to select files with common names and extensions. The default is *.*, which selects all files.

To Change the Selection Parameters for the File List Window

Version 6.0

[KEY]

1. Press **Alt-O** to display the Options menu.
2. Press **O** to choose the Modify Display command. The Modify Display submenu appears.

50 FILE SELECT FILTER

3. Press **S** to choose the File Select Filter command. The File Select Filter dialog box appears.

4. Type the selection parameters, using wildcards as desired. Press the **Tab** key to move from the Name field to the Extension field. Example: To list only .EXE program files, enter * in the Name field and **EXE** in the Extension field. Press the **Tab** key again.

5. Press **S** (for **S**elect) to accept the new selection parameters. (Pressing **Alt-S** replaces the last two actions.)

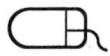

1. Pull down the Options menu, and choose the Modify Display command. The Modify Display submenu appears.

2. Choose the File Select Filter command. The File Select Filter dialog box appears.

3. Type the selection parameters, using wildcards as desired. Press the **Tab** key to move from the Name field to the Extension field. Example: To list only .EXE program files, enter * in the Name field and **EXE** in the Extension field.

4. Click on the Select button to accept the new selection parameters.

Shortcuts   Press **R** (for **R**eset) to reset the Name and Extension fields within the File Select Filter dialog box to *.*.

If you are using the keyboard, press the function key **F9** to immediately access the File Select Filter dialog box.

Version 5.5

1. Press **Alt-O** to display the Options menu.

2. Press **F** to choose the File Select Filter command. The File Select Filter dialog box appears.

FILE SELECT FILTER 51

3. Type the selection parameters, using wildcards as desired. Press the **Tab** key to move from the Name field to the Extension field. Example: To select only .EXE program files, enter * in the Name field and **EXE** in the Extension field. Press the **Tab** key again.

4. Press **S** (for **S**elect) to accept the new selection parameters. (Pressing **Alt-S** replaces the last two actions.)

1. Pull down the Options menu, and choose the File Select Filter command. The File Select Filter dialog box appears.

2. Type the selection parameters, using wildcards as desired. Press the **Tab** key to move from the Name field to the Extension field. Example: To list only .EXE program files, enter * in the Name field and **EXE** in the Extension field.

3. Click on the Select button to accept the new selection parameters.

Shortcuts Press **R** (for **R**eset) to reset the Name and Extension fields within the File Select Filter dialog box to *.*.

If you are using the keyboard, press the function key **F9** to immediately access the File Select Filter dialog box.

See Also *File Display Options, File List Filter, Unselect Files, Reset Selected Files.* The File Display Options command sets the information displayed for each file, as well as how the files are sorted in the File List window. The File List Filter command displays only those files that meet the file-name parameters you supply. You can use Unselect Files (version 6.0) and Reset Selected Files (version 5.5) to quickly unselect files highlighted with the File Select Filter command.

FIND
Version 5.5

See *Text Search*.

FORMAT DATA DISK

● **MENU**

Disk

● **PURPOSE** Formats a data disk in a floppy drive. Format Data Disk performs the same functions as the FORMAT command in DOS, but allows easier formatting without the use of cryptic command-line switches.

During formatting, the Format Data Disk command displays a progress indicator, showing tracks successfully (and, when applicable, unsuccessfully) formatted.

After formatting is complete, Shell always asks you to provide a volume name for the disk and asks whether you want to make the disk bootable. Both choices are optional.

Table 1.2 lists the disk formats supported by the Shell utility.

To Format a Disk

[KEY]

1. Press **Alt-D** to display the **D**isk menu.
2. Press **F** to choose the Format Data Disk command.

Table 1.2: Drive Types and Formats Supported by Shell

DISK SIZE	NO. OF SIDES	CAPACITY	NO. OF SECTORS	NO. OF TRACKS
5¼"	1	160K	8	40
5¼"	1	180K	9	40
5¼"	2	320K	8	40
5¼"	2	360K	9	40
5¼"	2	1.2Mb	15	80
3½"	2	720K	9	80
3½"	2	1.44Mb	18	80

3. Use ↑ and ↓ to select the drive you want to use for disk formatting, then press ↵. The Disk Initialization dialog box appears.

4. Press the number key that corresponds to the capacity of the disk you want to format. The available choices depend on the size, type, and capacity of the floppy-disk drives installed in your computer.

5. Place a blank disk in the appropriate drive.

6. Press **F** for Format to format the disk.

7. After the disk is formatted, provide a volume name (optional), and press ↵. Then, press **C** for Continue to go to the next step, or press **X** for Exit to return to Shell.

8. If you want to make the disk bootable (to use the disk to start the computer), press **B** (for Bootable). Otherwise, press **S** for Skip to go to the next step, or press **X** for Exit to return to Shell.

9. Shell displays the amount of formatted space on the disk, as well as any space allocated to bad sectors. Press **N** (for Next) to format the next disk, or press **X** (for Exit) to return to Shell.

At any time during disk formatting, you can cancel the operation by pressing the **F3** key.

FORMAT DATA DISK

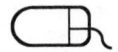

1. Pull down the Disk menu, and choose the Format Data Disk command.

2. Double-click on the drive you want to use for disk formatting. The Disk Initialization dialog box appears.

3. Click beside the capacity of the disk you want to format. The available choices depend on the size, type, and capacity of the floppy-disk drives in your computer.

4. Place a blank disk in the appropriate drive.

5. Click on the Format button to begin disk formatting.

6. After the disk is formatted, type a volume name (optional), and press ↵. Then, click on the Continue button to go to the next step, or click on the Exit button to return to Shell.

7. If you want to make the disk bootable (to use the disk to start the computer), click on the Bootable button. Otherwise, click on Skip to go to the next step, or click on Exit to return to Shell.

8. Shell displays the amount of formatted space on the disk, as well as any space allocated to bad sectors. Click on Next to format another disk, or click on Exit to return to Shell.

• **NOTES** During disk initialization, successfully formatted tracks are shown with a period. Tracks that could not be successfully formatted are shown with an E.

If you want to make a disk bootable, press **B** or click on the Bootable button when prompted to do so by Shell. The program sets aside the space necessary to make the disk bootable. At this point, however, the disk cannot yet be used to start your computer. You must complete the procedure by choosing the Make System Disk command, which copies the necessary system files to the newly formatted disk.

PC Tools also comes with PC Format, a stand-alone disk-formatting utility you can use at the DOS prompt.

HEX EDIT
Version 5.5

See *Hex Edit File*.

HEX EDIT FILE

● **MENU**

File

● **PURPOSE** Edits a file using hexadecimal (base 16) notation. The Hex Edit File command is normally used to edit binary files on a byte-by-byte basis.

To Use the Hex Editor

Version 6.0

[KEY]

1. Press **Alt-F** to display the File menu.
2. Press **F** to choose the Hex Edit File command. The Hex Edit window opens.
3. Edit the file, using the procedures detailed in the Notes section. Be sure to save your changes.
4. Press **F3** to exit.

56 HEX EDIT FILE

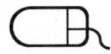

1. Pull down the File menu, and choose the Hex Edit File command. The Hex Edit window opens.
2. Edit the file, using the procedures detailed in the Notes section. Be sure to save your changes.
3. Click inside the Close box to exit.

Shortcut If you are using a mouse, you can activate any of the commands that appear along the bottom of the screen by clicking on them. For example, to save the file, merely click on Save.

• **NOTES** Shell initially shows the file in hex character display and View mode. You can toggle between ASCII and hex display by pressing the **F5** function key when in the View mode. If you don't see the data you want to edit, press any of the following keys to move within the file:

To Move	Press
Down one screen	PgDn
Up one screen	PgUp
To top of file	Home
To end of file	End

You can quickly move to any sector on your hard drive by pressing the **F6** function key. Type a new sector number, and press ↵ when you're finished.

To edit the file, position the cursor where you want to make the change, then press the **F7** function key to enter Edit mode. Type the new hexadecimal value; you can enter a string of new values. To save the edited file, press the **F5** function key from the Edit mode. While in Edit mode, you can switch between ASCII and hex display by pressing the **F8** function key.

HEX EDIT FILE

Version 5.5

[KEY]

1. Press **Alt-F** to display the File menu.
2. Press **H** to choose the Hex Edit command. The Hex Edit window opens.
3. Edit the file, using the procedures detailed in the Notes section. Be sure to save your changes.
4. Press **F3** to exit.

🖱

1. Pull down the File menu, and choose the Hex Edit command. The Hex Edit window opens.
2. Edit the file, using the procedures detailed in the Notes section. Be sure to save your changes.
3. Click inside the Close box to exit.

Shortcut If you are using a mouse, you can activate any of the commands that appear along the bottom of the screen by clicking on them. For example, to save the file, merely click on Save.

● **NOTES** Shell initially shows the file in hex character display and View mode. You can toggle between ASCII and hex display by pressing the **A** key when in the View mode. If you don't see the data you want to edit, press any of the following keys to move within the file:

To Move	Press
Down one screen	PgDn
Up one screen	PgUp
To top of file	Home
To end of file	End

You can quickly move to any sector on your hard drive by pressing S (for Change Sector). Type a new sector number, and press ↵ when you're finished.

To edit the file, position the cursor where you want to make the change, then press E to enter Edit mode. Type the new hexadecimal value; you can enter a string of new values. To save the edited file, press S from the Edit mode. While in Edit mode, you can switch between ASCII and hex display by pressing the F8 function key.

See Also *Edit File* (*File Edit* in version 5.5). Lets you edit an ASCII file using a text editor. If the file you're editing contains only standard text, use Edit File instead of Hex Edit File.

HIDE WINDOWS
Version 6.0 Only

● **MENU**

Options

● **PURPOSE** Hides all windows and menus (except for the shortcut function-key menu, shown at the very bottom of the screen). If the Background Mat option is turned off (as set with the Setup Configuration menu), the DOS screen is displayed. All Shell commands are still accessible, even though they are hidden from view.

To Hide All Windows and Menus

[KEY]

1. Press **Alt-O** to display the **O**ptions menu.
2. Press **W** to choose the Hide **W**indows command.

1. Pull down the Options menu.
2. Choose the Hide Windows command.

• **NOTES** The Hide Windows command is a toggle. With windows turned off, the command changes to Show Windows. Reselect the command to turn the windows back on.

See Also *Tree List Window, File List Window.* The Tree List Window command hides just the window(s) containing the directory tree. The File List Window command hides just the window(s) containing the file listing.

LAPLINK/QC
Version 6.0 Only

• **MENU**

Special

• **PURPOSE** Establishes a hard-wired communications link (through your computer's serial port) with a remote computer. The LapLink/QC command is normally used to connect to a laptop computer for downloading programs and files. Both the host and remote computers must be equipped with PC Tools 6.0 or LapLink Quick Connect software.

To Use LapLink

1. Press **Alt-S** to display the **S**pecial menu.
2. Press **L** to turn on LapLink/QC. Choose it again to turn it off.

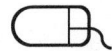

1. Pull down the Special menu.
2. Choose the LapLink/QC command to turn on LapLink. Choose the command again to turn it off.

● **NOTES** Be sure both computers are properly connected with a null-modem cable before choosing the LapLink/QC command.

LAUNCH
Version 6.0

● **MENU**

File

● **PURPOSE** Runs a program or batch file from Shell. After the program or batch file is completed, control returns to Shell. (In version 5.5, this command is called *Run*.)

To Run a Program or Batch File

1. In the File List window, select a program file (.EXE or .COM) or a batch file (.BAT) to run.
2. Press **Alt-F** to display the File menu.
3. Press **H** to choose the Launch command.
4. Provide any run-time parameters (option switches) that may be necessary for the program or batch file.

5. Press ↵ when you're finished.
6. Press **R** to run the program or batch file (or press **C** to cancel).

🖱

1. In the File List window, click on a program file (.EXE or .COM) or a batch file (.BAT) to run.
2. Pull down the File menu, and choose the Launch command.
3. Provide any run-time parameters (option switches) that may be necessary for the program or batch file.
4. Press ↵ when you're finished.
5. Click on the Run button to start the program or batch file (or click on the Cancel button).

Shortcut   The **Ctrl-↵** key combination is a shortcut for choosing the Launch command. Select a program or batch file to run, then press **Ctrl-↵**.

LOCATE FILE

● **MENU**

|6.0| File

|5.5| Disk

● **PURPOSE**   Locates files based on file-name specifications you provide. In version 6.0, you can narrow the search by also providing a text string to locate within the found files.

To Locate a File

Version 6.0

[KEY]

1. Press **Alt-F** to display the File menu.
2. Press **L** to choose the Locate File command.
3. Use the cursor keys to select Specify File Name (to search through all files), and press ↵.
4. Enter one or more file specifications to look for. You can include wildcards within the file names and extensions.
5. Press ↵ when you're finished.
6. Type an optional text string to search for (Shell will only search within those files previously specified). The text string can be up to 33 characters long.
7. Press ↵ when you're finished.

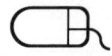

1. Pull down the File menu, and choose the Locate File command.
2. Double-click on Specify File Name (to search through all files).
3. Enter one or more file specifications to look for. You can include wildcards within the file names and extensions.
4. Press ↵ when you're finished.
5. Type an optional text string to search for (Shell will only search within those files previously specified). The text string can be up to 33 characters long.
6. Press ↵ when you're finished.

Shell displays files it has located that match your search criteria (if any) in a window.

LOCATE FILE

Shell gives you the option of searching all files (with the Specify File Name option) or just those document files that belong to a specific application. These additional file search options are provided based on the application programs originally found by PC Tools Deluxe during installation. (If no identifiable applications can be found, no additional file search options will be presented, so you can only select the Specify File Name option.) File ownership is based on file extensions, such as .DOC, .TXT, .WKS, and so forth. When searching for document files for a specific application, Shell only prompts you to enter a text string to search for.

Version 5.5

[KEY]

1. Press **Alt-D** to display the **D**isk menu.
2. Press **L** to choose the **L**ocate File command.
3. Type a name or wildcard for the file name.
4. Press ↵.
5. Type a name or wildcard for the file extension.
6. Press **Tab** to highlight the All option or Page at a Time option (depending on which one is currently active).
7. Press **A** to select **A**ll (all files are listed in a window), or press **P** to select **P**age at a Time (files are presented one page at a time).

1. Pull down the Disk menu, and choose the Locate File command.
2. Type a name or wildcard for the file name.
3. Press ↵.
4. Type a name or wildcard for the file extension.
5. Click on All (all files are listed in a window), or click on Page at a Time (files are presented one page at a time).
6. Press the ↵ key to start the search.

You can use wildcards in your search criteria, such as *.EXE. The wildcards function as they do within DOS.

Shell displays files it has located that match your search criteria (if any) in a window.

See Also   *Find* (version 5.5), *Text Search* (version 6.0). These commands look for specific text strings in previously selected files.

MAKE SYSTEM DISK

- **MENU**

Disk

- **PURPOSE**   Places necessary system files on a newly formatted disk so that the disk can be used to start (boot) the computer. **Important Note:** To successfully use the Make System Disk command, you must first format a disk using the Format Data Disk command and select the Bootable option. This clears necessary data space for the system files. You should not make a system disk if the disk already has data on it.

To Make a System Disk

[KEY]

1. Put a newly formatted disk in one of the floppy drives.
2. Press **Alt-D** to display the **D**isk menu.
3. Press **Y** to choose the Make System Disk command.
4. Use the cursor keys to select the drive that contains the disk.

5. Press the ↵ key.
6. Confirm that you want to make a system disk by pressing **S** (for **S**ystem), or press **X** for Exit to cancel the operation.
7. Shell now copies the necessary system files to the disk. Press **X** for Exit when the process is complete.

1. Put a newly formatted disk in one of the floppy drives.
2. Pull down the Disk menu, and choose the Make System Disk command.
3. Double-click on the drive that contains the disk.
4. Confirm that you want to make a system disk by clicking on the System button, or click on the Exit button to cancel the operation.
5. Shell now copies the necessary system files to the disk. Click on the Exit button when the process is complete.

See Also *Format Data Disk*. This command formats (initializes) a disk. Use this command before using Make System Disk.

MEMORY MAP

● **MENU**

Special

● **PURPOSE** Displays a list of programs loaded into memory and how much RAM is taken up by each.

To Display a Memory Map

[KEY]

1. Press **Alt-S** to display the Special menu.
2. Press **E** to choose the Memory Map command.
3. Press any one of the following keys:

    1   Shows only program memory blocks
    2   Shows only program memory blocks with hooked vectors
    3   Shows all memory blocks
    4   Shows all memory blocks with hooked vectors

4. Press **M** to display the map.
5. When viewing the map, press **N** to show the next page, or press **P** to show the previous page (if any). Press **X** to exit.

1. Pull down the Special menu, and choose the Memory Map command.
2. Click on any one of the following:

    1   Shows only program memory blocks
    2   Shows only program memory blocks with hooked vectors
    3   Shows all memory blocks
    4   Shows all memory blocks with hooked vectors

3. Click on the Map button to display the map.
4. When viewing the map, click on Next Page or Previous Page (if any). Click on Exit to leave the map.

• **NOTES**   *Program memory blocks* are segments of memory that contain currently "active" programs, including applications and terminate-and-stay-resident (TSR) programs. All memory blocks show usage of all memory locations, including those used by DOS. *Hooked vectors* are software entry points and their respective interrupt values.

See Also   *More File Info, Disk Info.* The More File Info command displays details about specific files, including the number of clusters that the file uses and its absolute starting cluster on the disk. The Disk Info command displays details about the currently active disk, such as number of files, total disk space, and amount of disk space still available.

MODIFY APPLICATIONS LIST

- **MENU**

    6.0 Applications

    5.5 Options

- **PURPOSE**   Adds or removes program entries on the Applications menu. (Version 6.0 uses a simplified approach, which does not use version 5.5's Modify Applications List command.)

To Add a New Program Entry

Version 6.0

1. Display the Applications menu (press **Alt-A** or click on Applications).
2. Press **F4** for Add a New Entry.
3. Use the cursor keys to select the location for the entry, and press ↵.

MODIFY APPLICATIONS LIST

4. Provide the required information in the entry blanks; press **Tab** to move from one field to the next.

5. When you are finished, press **F4** to accept the changes (or press **F3** to exit and cancel changes).

6. Repeat steps 1 through 5 to add another entry, or press **F3** to exit the Applications menu.

Version 5.5

[KEY]

1. Press **Alt-O** to display the Options menu.

2. Press **M** to choose the Modify Applications List command. The Modify Applications List dialog box appears.

3. Press **Alt-W** to add a New program entry.

4. Provide the required information in the entry blanks; press **Tab** to move from one field to the next.

5. When you are finished, press **Alt-O** to accept the changes.

6. Press **Alt-S** to save the new entry.

7. Press **Alt-X** to exit the Modify Applications List window.

1. Pull down the Options menu, and choose the Modify Applications List command. The Modify Applications List dialog box appears.

2. Click on the New button.

3. Provide the required information in the entry blanks; press **Tab** to move from one field to the next.

4. When you are finished, press OK to accept the changes.

5. Click on the Save button to record the new entry.

MODIFY APPLICATIONS LIST 69

6. Click on the Exit button to leave the Modify Applications List window.

To Edit an Existing Program Entry

Version 6.0

1. Display the Applications menu (press **Alt-A** or click on Applications).
2. Press **F5** to edit an existing entry.
3. Use the cursor keys to select the entry you want to edit, and press ↵.
4. Change the desired information in the entry blanks; press **Tab** to move from one field to the next.
5. When you are finished, press **F4** to accept the changes (or press **F3** to exit and cancel changes).
6. Repeat steps 1 through 5 to edit another entry, or press **F3** to exit the Applications menu.

Version 5.5

[KEY]

1. Press **Alt-O** to display the Options menu.
2. Press **M** to choose the Modify Applications List command. The Modify Applications List dialog box appears.
3. Press **Alt-N** (for Next) until the program entry you want is displayed (press **Alt-P** to display the Previous entry).
4. Press **Alt-E** to edit the entry.
5. Change the required information in the entry blanks; press **Tab** to move from one field to the next.
6. When you are finished, press **Alt-O** to accept the changes.
7. Press **Alt-S** to save the new entry.
8. Press **Alt-X** to exit the Modify Applications List window.

70 MODIFY APPLICATIONS LIST

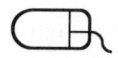

1. Pull down the Options menu, and choose the Modify Applications List command. The Modify Applications List dialog box appears.
2. Click on the Next button until the program entry you want is displayed (or click on the Previous button to look at the previous entry).
3. Click on the Edit button to edit the entry.
4. Change the required information in the entry blanks; press **Tab** to move from one field to the next.
5. Click on the OK button to accept the changes, then click on the Save button to record the entry.
6. Click on the Exit button to leave the Modify Applications List window.

To Delete a Program Entry

Version 6.0

1. Display the Applications menu (press **Alt-A** or click on Applications).
2. Press **F6** to delete an entry.
3. Use the cursor keys to select the entry you want to delete, and press ↵.
4. Press ↵ to delete, or press **Alt-X** to exit.
5. Repeat steps 1 through 4 to delete another entry, or press **F3** to exit the Applications menu.

Version 5.5

1. Press **Alt-O** to display the Options menu.

2. Press **M** to choose the **M**odify Applications List command. The Modify Applications List dialog box appears.
3. Press **Alt-N** (for **N**ext) until the program entry you want is displayed (press **Alt-P** to display the **P**revious entry).
4. Press **Alt-D** to delete the entry.
5. Press **Alt-S** to save the deletion.
6. Press **Alt-X** to exit the Modify Applications List window.

1. Pull down the Options menu, and choose the Modify Applications List command. The Modify Applications List dialog box appears.
2. Click on the Next button until the program entry you want is displayed (click on the Previous button to display the previous entry).
3. Click on the Delete button to erase the entry.
4. Click on the Save button to make the deletion permanent.
5. Click on the Exit button to leave the Modify Applications List window.

MODIFY DISPLAY
Version 6.0 Only

● **MENU**

Options

● **PURPOSE**   Submenu for eight commands for controlling the appearance of the Shell display.

To Display the Modify Display Submenu

[KEY]

1. Press **Alt-O** to display the Options menu.
2. Press **O** to choose the Modify Display command. The Modify Display submenu appears.

You can now select a command on the submenu.

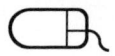

1. Pull down the Options menu.
2. Choose the Modify Display command. The Modify Display submenu appears.

You can now select a command on the submenu.

● **NOTES** The Modify Display submenu contains the following commands:

Command	Menu Selection Key	Shortcut Key
Tree/Files Switch	T	Tab
Two List Display	W	Ins
One List Display	O	Del
Active List Switch	A	
File List Filter	L	
File Select Filter	S	
File Display Options	D	
Unselect Files	U	

See the individual entries for these commands for more information on how to use them.

MORE FILE INFO

● **MENU**

File

● **PURPOSE** Displays useful "at-a-glance" information about a selected file, including file size, date/time of creation or last edit, and current file attributes.

To Display Information about a File

[KEY]

1. Select a file to view.
2. Press **Alt-F** to display the File menu.
3. Press **I** to choose the More File Info command. The More File Info information box appears.
4. Press **X** for Exit when you're finished.

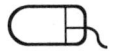

1. Click on a file to view.
2. Pull down the File menu, and choose the More File Info command. The More File Info information box appears.
3. Click on the Exit button when you're finished.

Shortcut You can easily view information in several files by selecting those files, then choosing the More File Info command. Press **N** (or click on the Next button) to display the information for the next file.

MOVE FILE

- **NOTES** The More File Info information box displays the following information about the selected file:

  - File name
  - Extension
  - File path (disk and directory path)
  - File attributes
  - Last time file accessed (this actually displays date and time file was created or last edited, not accessed)
  - File length
  - Total clusters occupied by file
  - Starting cluster number
  - Total number of files contained in the same directory as the selected file

MOVE
Version 5.5

See *Move File*.

MOVE FILE

- **MENU**

File

- **PURPOSE** Moves one or more selected files to a different disk or directory.

To Move a File

[KEY]

1. Select the disk and directory that holds the file you want to move.
2. Use the cursor keys in the File List window to highlight the file you want to move.
3. Press **Alt-F** to display the File menu.
4. Press **M** to choose the Move File command.
5. Confirm the move by pressing **C** (for Continue), or press **X** for Exit.
6. Use the cursor keys to select the drive where you want to move the file.
7. Select a subdirectory for the file, if any, using the cursor keys.
8. Press ↵. The file is moved to the indicated drive and directory.

1. Select the disk and directory that holds the file you want to move.
2. In the File List window, click on the file you want to move.
3. Pull down the File menu, and choose the Move File command.
4. Click on Continue to proceed with the file move, or click on Exit to cancel.
5. Click on the drive where you want to move the file.
6. Select a subdirectory for the file, if any.

Shortcut If you are using a mouse, you can "drag move" files. The procedure works best in Two List Display.

1. In one list, select the disk and directory that contains the file you want to move.

2. In the other list, select the disk and directory where you want to move the file.
3. Click on the file you want to move.
4. Press the **Ctrl** key and keep it depressed during the next two steps.
5. While holding down the left mouse button, drag the mouse pointer into the destination File List window.
6. Release the mouse button and **Ctrl** key.

As you drag the mouse with the file in tow, Shell indicates that you are moving one or more files. This technique works only when you move files from one disk or directory to another.

● **NOTES** You can move more than one file at a time, using any of the three methods outlined above. Select all the files you want to move, then follow the same steps you would use to move a single file.

See Also   *Copy File*. Copies files between directories and disks.

ONE LIST DISPLAY

● **MENU**

| 6.0 | Options➤Modify Display

| 5.5 | Options

● **PURPOSE** Displays the contents of a single disk and directory. The directory structure is shown in the Tree window; the files are shown in the File List window.

ONE LIST DISPLAY 77

To Display a Single Disk and Directory

Version 6.0

[KEY]

1. Press **Alt-O** to display the **O**ptions menu.
2. Press **O** to choose the M**o**dify Display command. The Modify Display submenu appears.
3. From the Modify Display submenu, press **O** to choose the **O**ne List Display command.

🖱

1. Pull down the Options menu, and choose the Modify Display command. The Modify Display submenu appears.
2. From the Modify Display submenu, choose the One List Display command.

Shortcut You can press the **Ins** key to choose the One List Display command.

Version 5.5

[KEY]

1. Press **Alt-O** to display the **O**ptions menu.
2. Press **O** to choose the **O**ne List Display command.

🖱

1. Pull down the Options menu.
2. Choose the One List Display command.

Shortcut You can press the **Ins** key to choose the One List Display command.

See Also   *Two List Display*. Displays two sets of Tree/File List windows.

PARK DISK

- **MENU**

Disk

- **PURPOSE**   Parks the heads of the hard disk. Shell places the magnetic heads at a normally unused portion of the hard drive to help minimize data loss due to hard-disk crashes. (A hard-disk crash is most likely to occur when you move your computer.)

To Park the Hard Disk

[KEY]

1. Press **Alt-D** to display the **D**isk menu.
2. Press **P** to choose the **P**ark Disk command.

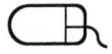

1. Pull down the Disk menu.
2. Choose the Park Disk command.

- **NOTES**   You can cancel the Park Disk command, even after you've selected it, by choosing Cancel in the Park Disk information box. This is helpful if you've accidentally selected the command and want to return to Shell.

PRINT DIRECTORY
Version 5.5

See *Print File List*.

PRINT FILE

● **MENU**

File

● **PURPOSE** Prints the contents of a file. You can choose to print the file using standard defaults for margins and line settings, or choose your own settings to format the document. The Print File command is normally used to print ASCII-only text documents, but it can also be used to print binary files, showing both ASCII and hexadecimal values.

To Print a File

[KEY]

1. Select a file in the File List window that you want to print.
2. Press **Alt-F** to display the File menu.
3. Press **P** to choose the Print File command. The File Print dialog box appears.
4. Select one of the three print options (detailed in the Notes section), then press **R** to initiate printing. You can also press **N** to choose the next file (if you selected more than one file), or press **C** to cancel printing.

PRINT FILE

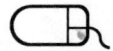

1. Select a file in the File List window that you want to print.
2. Pull down the File menu, and choose the Print File command. The File Print dialog box appears.
3. Select one of the three print options (detailed in the Notes section), then click on the Print button to initiate printing. You can also click on the Next button to go to the next file (if you selected more than one file), or click on Cancel to stop printing.

• **NOTES** Prior to printing, you should select one of the three options in the the File Print dialog box. Press the appropriate key as shown:

- **P**rint as standard text file: prints text with standard margins only.
- Print file using PC Shell print **o**ptions: prints text only using setup options you provide (see below).
- **D**ump each sector in ASCII and HEX: prints file showing ASCII and hexadecimal values for each byte.

If you choose to print with options, Shell displays an additional dialog box where you can set the following:

Option	Default
Lines per page	66
Margin lines top and bottom	4
Extra spaces between lines	0
Left margin	01
Right margin	080
Page headings (Yes or No response)	N
Page footings (Yes or No response)	N
Page numbers (Yes or No response)	N

PRINT FILE LIST 81

Option — **Default**

Want to stop between pages? (Yes or No) — N

Want to eject last page? (Yes or No) — Y

To set any option, press the appropriate cursor keys to highlight the option, then type the new setting. Press ↵ when you're finished. To print the file, press **P** or click on Print.

See Also *Print File List.* Prints the current directory.

PRINT FILE LIST

● **MENU**

File

● **PURPOSE** Prints a list of files from the currently selected disk and directory. (In version 5.5, this command is called *Print Directory*.)

To Print a List of Files

[KEY]

1. Select the drive and/or directory to print.
2. Press **Alt-F** to display the File menu.
3. Press **T** to choose the Print File List command (in version 5.5, the command is called Print Directory).

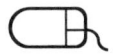

1. Select the drive and/or directory to print.

2. Pull down the File menu, and choose the Print File List command (in version 5.5, the command is called Print Directory).

● **NOTES** Before using the Print File List command, be sure the printer is turned on and is online. Shell displays an error message if the printer is not ready.

See Also   *Print File.* Prints the contents of individual files.

QUICK FILE VIEW
Version 6.0

● **MENU**

File

● **PURPOSE** Displays the contents of the currently selected file. You can view ASCII files, binary files, and document files created by other applications. You can only view the contents of the file; you cannot edit the file. When you view documents created by various applications, such as dBASE or Lotus 1-2-3, Shell presents them properly formatted. Version 6.0 supports over 30 document types, detailed in the Notes section. (In version 5.5, this command is called *View.*)

To View a File

KEY

1. Select a file to view.
2. Press **Alt-F** to display the File menu.
3. Press **Q** to choose the Quick File View command. The Viewer window appears.

QUICK FILE VIEW

4. When you are finished viewing the document, press the **F3** function key to exit the Viewer window.

1. Select a file to view.

2. Pull down the File menu, and choose the Quick File View command. The Viewer window appears.

3. When you are finished viewing the document, click inside the Close box in the upper-left corner of the Viewer window.

Shortcut If you are going to view several different files, select them all, then press the **F9** function key to move to the next one in the selection.

• **NOTES** The Default Viewer command (on the Setup Configuration submenu under the Options menu) selects how the Quick File View feature normally displays files.

- When set to TEXT, files are shown in ASCII format.
- When set to BINARY, files are shown in both ASCII and hexadecimal format.

Press any of the following keys to see more of the document in the Viewer window:

To	Press
Move to top of document	Home
Move to end of document	End
Move down one page	PgDn
Move up one page	PgUp

You can contract (unzoom) the Viewer window by pressing the **F8** function key. Press **F8** again to return the screen to full size. Once you have unzoomed the window, choose the View Window command (on the Options menu) to turn the window OFF.

Version 6.0 comes with additional file filters to view documents created with a variety of applications, including WordStar,

84 QUICK FILE VIEW

WordPerfect, Excel, and several dozen others. Table 1.3 lists those documents Shell can display in proper format.

Table 1.3: File Filters Used with Quick View

WORD PROCESSOR VIEWERS	DATABASE VIEWERS
Text (default)	Clipper
DisplayWrite	dBASE
Microsoft Windows Write	dBXL
Microsoft Word	FoxBASE
Microsoft Works	Microsoft Works
MultiMate	Paradox
PC Tools Desktop Notepads	R:BASE
WordPerfect	
WordStar (3.3 and later versions)	
WordStar 2000	
XyWrite	

SPREADSHEET VIEWERS	MISC. FILE VIEWERS
Borland Quattro	ARC
Lotus 1-2-3	Binary
Lotus Symphony	LHARC
Microsoft Excel	.PAK
Microsoft Works	.PCX
Mosaic Twin	PKZIP
MultiPlan	ZOO
VP Planner Plus	
Words and Figures	

Notes: Shell displays the file in binary format if the file has a .COM, .EXE, .OBJ, .BIN, or .SYS file extension. If the file is in one of the formats listed above and has the extension .TXT or .BAT, Shell displays it in text mode.

QUICK RUN

Version 5.5 Only

• MENU

Options

• PURPOSE
Keeps Shell in RAM while other applications are being run.

- When Quick Run is turned on (a check mark appears beside the command), Shell is retained in memory when another program is launched. When the program terminates, Shell is reactivated more quickly.

- When Quick Run is turned off (no check mark appears beside the command), Shell is flushed from memory when another program is launched. When the program terminates, Shell must be reloaded into memory, which takes extra time.

When possible, keep Quick Run on, unless your applications require extra memory to operate properly.

The Quick Run command is available only in version 5.5 and is not present when you run Shell in resident mode (loaded with the /R option switch).

To Change the Quick Run Setting

KEY

1. Press **Alt-O** to display the **O**ptions menu.
2. Press **Q** to turn **Q**uick Run on or off, as desired.

1. Pull down the Options menu.

2. Choose the Quick Run command.

RENAME
Version 5.5

See *Rename File*.

RENAME FILE

- **MENU**

File

- **PURPOSE** Renames the selected file.

To Rename a File

[KEY]

1. Select the file you want to rename.
2. Press **Alt-F** to display the File menu.
3. Press **R** to choose the Rename File command. The File Rename dialog box appears.
4. Enter the new file name and extension in the blanks provided (press ↵ or ↓ after entering each).
5. Press **R** to rename the file, or press **C** to cancel the operation.

1. Select the file you want to rename.
2. Pull down the File menu, and choose the Rename File command. The File Rename dialog box appears.
3. Enter the new file name and extension in the blanks provided (press ↵ or ↓ after entering each).
4. Click on the Rename button, or click on the Cancel button.

RENAME VOLUME

- **MENU**

Disk

- **PURPOSE**   Renames the disk volume label.

To Rename the Disk Volume Label

1. Activate the disk you want to rename (press **Ctrl** and the drive letter, such as **Ctrl-A** for drive A).
2. Press **Alt-D** to display the Disk menu.
3. Press **R** to choose the Rename Volume command. The Disk Rename dialog box appears.
4. Type the new name in the blank (up to 11 characters), and press ↵ or ↓.
5. Press **R** for Rename, or press **C** for Cancel.

1. Activate the disk you want to rename by clicking on the drive letter above the Tree window.
2. Pull down the Disk menu, and choose the Rename Volume command. The Disk Rename dialog box appears.
3. Type the new name in the blank (up to 11 characters), and Press ↵ or ↓.
4. Click on the Rename button, or click on the Cancel button.

RE-READ THE TREE

• **MENU**

Options

• **PURPOSE** Forces Shell to reread the disk directory and files so that any last-minute changes are accurately displayed in the Tree and File List windows.

To Force Shell to Reread the DOS Tree

1. Press **Alt-O** to display the **O**ptions menu.
2. Press **D** to choose the Re-Rea**d** the Tree command.

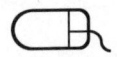

1. Pull down the Options menu.
2. Choose the Re-Read the Tree command.

RESET SELECTED FILES
Version 5.5

See *Unselect Files*.

RUN
Version 5.5

- **MENU**

File

- **PURPOSE** Runs a program or batch file from Shell. After the program or batch file is completed, control returns to Shell. (In version 6.0, this command is called *Launch*.)

To Run a Program or Batch File

[KEY]

1. In the File List window, select a program file (.EXE or .COM) or a batch file (.BAT) to run.
2. Press **Alt-F** to display the File menu.
3. Press **N** to choose the Run command.
4. Provide any run-time parameters (option switches) that may be necessary for the program or batch file.
5. Press ↵ when you're finished.
6. Press **R** to run the program or batch file (or press **C** to cancel).

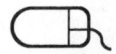

1. In the File List window, click on a program file (.EXE or .COM) or a batch file (.BAT) to run.
2. Pull down the File menu, and choose the Run command.
3. Provide any run-time parameters (option switches) that may be necessary for the program or batch file.
4. Press ↵ when you're finished.
5. Click on the Run button to start the program or batch file (or click on the Cancel button).

Shortcut The **Ctrl-↵** key combination is a shortcut for choosing the Run command. Select a program or batch file to run, then press **Ctrl-↵**.

● **NOTES** The setting of the Quick Run command (found on the Options menu) determines how Shell is retained in memory when the program or batch file is executed. Turn on Quick Run if you have enough memory to run the program or batch file; otherwise, turn it off. When turned off, it will take a while longer for Shell to return when the program or batch file is finished. Note that version 6.0 of PC Tools does not have the Quick Run command.

See Also *Quick Run* (version 5.5 only). Determines how Shell is retained in memory while the program or batch file is being executed.

SAVE CONFIGURATION
Version 5.5

See *Save Configuration File*.

SAVE CONFIGURATION FILE

● **MENU**

Options

● **PURPOSE** Records changes you make to the display and configuration settings of Shell, as made with the commands on the Options menu.

To Use Save Configuration File

[KEY]

1. Press **Alt-O** to display the Options menu.
2. Press **A** (version 6.0) or **S** (version 5.5) to choose the Save Configuration command.

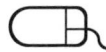

1. Pull down the Options menu.
2. Choose the Save Configuration command.

SCREEN COLORS

● **MENU**

|6.0| Options➤Setup Configuration

SCREEN COLORS

5.5 Options

- **PURPOSE** Modifies the screen colors according to your selection. You can change the colors of the menu bar, window, dialog box, and message box.

To Change the Screen Colors

Version 6.0

[KEY]

1. Press **Alt-O** to display the **O**ptions menu.
2. Press **C** to choose the Setup **C**onfiguration command. The Setup Configuration submenu appears.
3. Press **S** to choose the **S**creen Colors command. The Color Change dialog box appears.
4. Make your color selections as described in the Notes section, and press ↵ to accept the changes.

1. Pull down the Options menu, and choose the Setup Configuration command. The Setup Configuration submenu appears.
2. Choose the Screen Colors command. The Color Change dialog box appears.
3. Make your color selections as described in the Notes section, and click on the OK button to accept the changes.

Version 5.5

[KEY]

1. Press **Alt-O** to display the **O**ptions menu.

2. Press **C** to choose the Screen Colors command. The Color Change dialog box appears.

3. Make your color selections as described in the Notes section, and press ↵ to accept the changes.

1. Pull down the Options menu, and choose the Screen Colors command. The Color Change dialog box appears.

2. Make your color selections as described in the Notes section, and click on the OK button to accept the changes.

• **NOTES** You can change the color of the following elements of the Shell display by pressing the appropriate key:

Element	Key
Menu Bar Background	B
Menu Bar Foreground	F
Selected Menu Items	N
Window Background	A
Window Foreground	G
Window Selected Data	T
Dialog Box Background	D
Dialog Box Foreground	R
Message Box Background	K
Message Box Foreground	E

The following color choices are available for each element of the Shell display (not all colors are available with all monitor types):

Color	Key
Black	0
Blue	1
Green	2
Cyan	3
Red	4

Color	Key
Magenta	5
Orange	6
White	7

- Press **H** to turn on **H**igh Intensity for any of the above colors.
- Press **I** to set High Intensity ON when leaving Shell (often necessary when using an EGA display).
- If you have version 6.0, press **L** to set the display for use with a laptop LCD screen.
- If you have version 6.0, press **W** to set the display to black and white.

You can return to the default color scheme by pressing **S** (for Re**s**et).

SEARCH DISK

● **MENU**

Disk

● **PURPOSE** Searches the entire disk (including data for files that have been previously erased) for the text string you specify. The search is not case sensitive: **TEST** finds *test, Test, TEST,* and other variations.

To Search a Disk

[KEY]

1. Press **Alt-D** to display the **D**isk menu.

2. Press **S** to choose the Search Disk command. The Disk Search dialog box appears.

3. Type the string you want to search for (up to 32 characters).

4. Press ↵ when you're finished.

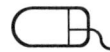

1. Pull down the Disk menu, and choose the Search Disk command. The Disk Search dialog box appears.

2. Type the string you want to search for (up to 32 characters).

3. Press ↵ when you're finshed.

• **NOTES** The search through the entire disk may take seconds or several minutes, depending on the size of the disk (searching takes longest with large hard-disk drives).

When Shell finds a match, the following additional commands appear:

Version 6.0

Command	Action	Press
Help	Help on Search Disk	F1
Index	Help index	F2
Exit	Return to Shell	F3
Search	Finds next occurrence	F7
Name	Displays file name	F8
Edit	Edit window	F9

Version 5.5

Command	Action	Press
Continue Disk Search	Finds next occurrence	C
Show Filename	Displays file name	F
Edit Sector	Displays Edit window	E

If the search string is not part of a valid file (such as a directory name), Shell displays the directory where the string occurs when you use the Name command (in version 6.0) or the Show Filename command (in version 5.5).

You can stop the disk search at any time by pressing **Esc** or the **F3** function key.

See Also   *Text Search* (version 6.0), *Find* (version 5.5). These commands find a text string in one or more specified files. The *Locate File* command finds files by name.

SETUP CONFIGURATION
Version 6.0 Only

● MENU

Options

● PURPOSE
Submenu under the Options menu for an additional ten commands. These commands allow you to customize Shell to your own requirements. The commands on the Setup Configuration submenu are the following:

- *Change User Levels:* Switches user level between Beginning, Intermediate, and Advanced.

- *Short Cut Keys:* Turns display of shortcut keys on and off.

- *DOS Command Line:* Turns display of DOS command line on and off.

- *Wait on DOS Screen:* When turned on, pauses screen after completion of a DOS command. When turned off, Shell restarts immediately.

- *Background Mat:* Turns background pattern on and off.

- *Viewer Cfg.* (configuration): Changes orientation of View window between vertical and horizontal.

SETUP CONFIGURATION

- *Default Viewer:* Sets default display (either text or binary) for nonsupported file types.
- *Screen Colors:* Sets screen colors.
- *Date/Time:* Sets current date and time.
- *Define Function Keys:* Reassigns function keys.

To Use the Setup Configuration Submenu

[KEY]

1. Press **Alt-O** to display the Options menu.
2. Press **C** to choose the Setup Configuration command. The Setup Configuration submenu appears.
3. Press one of the following keys to choose a command on the Setup Configuration submenu:

U	Change **U**ser Level
K	Short Cut **K**eys
C	DOS **C**ommand Line
W	**W**ait on DOS Screen
B	**B**ackground Mat
V	**V**iewer Cfg.
D	**D**efault Viewer
S	**S**creen Colors
T	Date/**T**ime
F	Define **F**unction Keys

1. Pull down the Options menu, and choose the Setup Configuration command. The Setup Configuration submenu appears.

2. Click on one of the commands on the Setup Configuration submenu.

● **NOTES** All the commands under Setup Configuration change the operation or appearance of Shell in some way. The defaults for the Setup Configuration settings are indicated in Table 1.4.

Table 1.4: Setup Configuration Defaults

COMMAND	DEFAULT SETTING
Change User Level	Advanced
Short Cut Keys	OFF
DOS Command Line	ON
Wait on DOS Screen	ON
Background Mat	OFF
Viewer Cfg.	VERT
Default Viewer	BINARY
Screen Colors	See *Screen Colors*
Date/Time	Set by DOS
Define Function Keys	See *Define Function Keys*

SHORT CUT KEYS
Version 6.0 Only

● **MENU**

Options➤Setup Configuration

● **PURPOSE** Turns the shortcut keys menu that appears at the bottom of the display on or off.

To Turn the Shortcut Keys Menu On or Off

[KEY]

1. Press **Alt-O** to display the **O**ptions menu.
2. Press **C** to choose the Setup **C**onfiguration command. The Setup Configuration submenu appears. The current setting of the Short Cut Keys command is shown as ON or OFF.
3. Press **K** to choose the Short Cut **K**eys command. The new setting of the command (either ON or OFF) is shown.
4. Press the **F3** function key to exit the menu.

1. Pull down the Options menu, and choose the Setup Configuration command. The Setup Configuration submenu appears. The current setting of the Short Cut Keys command is shown as ON or OFF.
2. Click on the Short Cut Keys command. The new setting of the command (either ON or OFF) is shown.
3. Click anywhere outside the menu to go back to Shell.

SIZE/MOVE WINDOW

- **MENU**

Options

- **PURPOSE** Moves and resizes the active window within the display.

To Move and Resize the Active Window

[KEY]

1. Highlight the window you want to move or size.
2. Press **Alt-O** to display the **O**ptions menu.
3. Press **S** (version 6.0) or **Z** (version 5.5) to choose the Size/Move Window command.
4. Press S to size the window, or press M to move the window.
5. Use the cursor keys to move or size the window as desired.
6. Press ↵ when you're finished.

- To move the window, position the mouse pointer on the top border and drag it to its new location. To resize the window, position the mouse pointer in the lower-right corner and drag.

Shortcut Press **Alt** and **spacebar** in tandem to choose the Size/Move Window command quickly.

SYSTEM INFO

● **MENU**

Special

● **PURPOSE** Displays important information about your computer, as set by the DIP switches and/or the SETUP parameters within your computer. Note that the System Info command can display incorrect information if your computer is set up improperly.

To Display Information about Your System

[KEY]

1. Press **Alt-S** to display the **S**pecial menu.
2. Press **S** to choose the **S**ystem Info command. The System Information box appears.
3. Press **F3** or **Esc** to return to Shell.

1. Pull down the Special menu, and choose the System Info command. The System Information box appears.
2. Click inside the Close box to return to Shell.

● **NOTES** The System Info command displays the following information, where appropriate:

- *Computer:* type, such as XT or AT.
- *BIOS programs dated:* copyright date impressed on the motherboard BIOS chip(s).
- *Operating system:* type of operating system, such as DOS, and version.
- *Number of logical disk drives:* number of default drives, as set by DOS (*not* necessarily the number actually contained in your computer).
- *Logical drive letter range:* drive letters (A, B, C, etc.), as set by DOS (*not* necessarily the drives actually contained in your computer).
- *Serial Ports:* number of active serial ports, if any.
- *Parallel Ports:* number of active parallel ports, if any.
- *CPU Type:* type of CPU, such as 80286 or 80386.
- *Relative speed (orig PC = 100%):* a test of the speed, in percent, of your computer, calculated relative to the original 4.77 MHz IBM PC.

- *Math co-processor present:* indicates whether your computer is equipped with a math coprocessor.
- *User programs are loaded at HEX paragraph:* memory location, in hexadecimal format, of first user program in RAM.
- *Memory used by DOS and resident programs:* amount of base RAM, in bytes, used by the system and TSR-type programs.
- *Memory available for user programs:* amount of base RAM, in bytes, left free for programs.
- *Total memory reported by DOS:* amount of base RAM, in kilobytes, as reported by DOS.
- *PC Shell has found the total memory to be:* amount of base RAM, in kilobytes, according to Shell.
- *Video adapter:* type, operating mode, and installed memory.
- *Expanded memory total:* amount of RAM installed for expanded memory and kilobytes used (if applicable).
- *Extended memory total:* amount of RAM installed for extended memory, and kilobytes used (if applicable).
- *Additional ROM BIOS found at HEX paragraph:* memory location, in hexadecimal format, of additional ROM BIOS program.

See Also *More File Info, Disk Info.* The More Info File command provides details about individual files. The Disk Info command provides details (including capacity and space available) about the current disk.

TEXT SEARCH

• MENU

File

TEXT SEARCH

- **PURPOSE**   Searches files to find a text string you specify. The text string can contain up to 32 characters. You can search through all files in the current directory, or you can limit the search only to selected or unselected files within the current directory. (This command is called *Find* in version 5.5.)

To Search Files for a Text String

Version 6.0

KEY

1. Select one or more files to search for, if desired.
2. Press **Alt-F** to display the File menu.
3. Press **S** to choose the Text **S**earch command. The File Search dialog box appears.
4. Type the text string to search for. If the Select and If Found options meet your approval, press ↵ to start the search (go to step 9). If not, press **Tab** to select the Search options, and go to step 5.
5. Press one of the following keys:
   - **A** to search through all files (you can't use this if you previously selected files).
   - **S** to search through selected files only.
   - **U** to search through unselected files only.
6. Press **Tab** to move to the If Found options.
7. Press one of the following keys:
   - **S** to select each found file and continue the search (you can't use this if you previously selected files).
   - **P** to pause after each successful find.
8. Press ↵ to start the search.
9. If Shell finds a match, and you have selected to pause after each successful search, the file name that contains the text string is displayed. You have five options:
   - Press **F3** to exit.

104 TEXT SEARCH

- Press **F6** to select the file (you can do this only if you've chosen to search unselected files).
- Press **F7** to restart the search (the string may be found two or more times within the same file).
- Press **F8** to edit the file.
- Press **F9** to go to the next file.

10. You can stop the search at any time by pressing the **F3** function key.

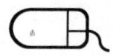

1. Select one or more files to search for, if desired.
2. Pull down the File menu, and choose the Find command. The File Search dialog box appears.
3. Type the text string to search for. If the Select and If Found options meet your approval, press ↵ to start the search (go to step 8). If not, press **Tab** to select the Search options, and go to step 4.
4. Click on one of the following:
    - *All files* to look through all files in the current directory (you can't use this if you previously selected files).
    - *Selected files* to search through selected files only.
    - *Unselected files* to search through only those files that are not selected.
5. Press **Tab** to move to the If Found options.
6. Click on one of the following:
    - *Select file and continue* to select each found file and continue the search (you can't use this if you previously selected files).
    - *Pause search* to stop the search after each successful find.
7. Press ↵ to start the search.
8. If Shell finds a match, and you have selected to pause after each successful search, the file name that contains the text string is displayed. You have five options:
    - Click on Exit to exit.

- Click on Select to select the file.
- Click on Search to restart the search.
- Click on Edit to edit the file.
- Click on Nextf to go to the next file and resume searching.

9. You can stop the search at any time by pressing the **F3** function key.

Version 5.5

[KEY]

1. Select one or more files to search for, if desired.

2. Press **Alt-F** to display the File menu.

3. Press **F** to choose the Find command. The File Search dialog box appears.

4. Type the text string to search for. If the Select and If Found options meet your approval, press ↵ to start the search (go to step 9). If not, press **Tab** to select the Search options, and go to step 5.

5. Press one of the following keys:
- **A** to search through all files (you can't use this if you previously selected files).
- **S** to search through selected files only.
- **U** to search through unselected files only.

6. Press **Tab** to move to the If Found options.

7. Press one of the following keys:
- **S** to select each found file and continue the search (you can't use this if you previously selected files).
- **P** to pause after each successful find.

8. Press ↵ to start the search.

9. If Shell finds a match, and you have selected to pause after each successful search, the file name that contains the text string is displayed. You have four options:
- Press **C** to continue the search.

106 TEXT SEARCH

- Press **V** to view the file.
- Press **E** to edit the file.
- Press **N** to find the next file.

10. You can stop the search at any time by pressing the **F3** function key.

1. Select one or more files to search for, if desired.
2. Pull down the File menu, and choose the Find command. The File Search dialog box appears.
3. Type the text string to search for. If the Select and If Found options meet your approval, press ↵ to start the search (go to step 8). If not, press **Tab** to select the Search options, and go to step 4.
4. Click on one of the following:
   - *All files* to look through all files in the current directory (you can't use this if you previously selected files).
   - *Selected files* to search through selected files only.
   - *Unselected files* to search through only those files that are not selected.
5. Press **Tab** to move to the If Found options.
6. Click on one of the following:
   - *Select file and continue* to select each found file and continue the search (you can't use this if you previously selected files).
   - *Pause search* to stop the search after each successful find.
7. Press ↵ to start the search.
8. If Shell finds a match, and you have selected to pause after each successful search, the file name that contains the text string is displayed. You have four options:
   - Click on *Continue search* to go on.
   - Click on *View file* to look at the file.
   - Click on *Edit file* to edit the file.

- Click on *Next file* to go to the next file.
9. You can stop the search at any time by pressing the **F3** function key.

TREE/FILES SWITCH

- **MENU**

  6.0 Options➤Modify Display

  5.5 Options

- **PURPOSE** Switches the active window between the Tree and File List windows.

To Switch the Active Window

Version 6.0

[KEY]

1. Press **Alt-O** to display the Options menu.
2. Press **O** to choose the Modify Display command. The Modify Display submenu appears.
3. Press **T** to choose the Tree/Files Switch command.

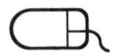

1. Pull down the Options menu, and choose the Modify Display command. The Modify Display submenu appears.
2. Choose the Tree/Files Switch command.

Shortcut Press the **Tab** key to switch quickly between the Tree and File List windows.

Version 5.5

[KEY]

1. Press **Alt-O** to display the **O**ptions menu.
2. Press **T** to choose the Tree/Files Switch command.

🖱

1. Pull down the Options menu.
2. Choose the Tree/Files Switch command.

Shortcut Press the **Tab** key to switch quickly between the Tree and File List windows.

TREE LIST WINDOW
Version 6.0 Only

● **MENU**

Options

● **PURPOSE** Turns the Tree window on and off. The current setting (either ON or OFF) of the window is shown beside the Tree List Window command on the Options menu.

To Turn the Tree Window On or Off

[KEY]

1. Press **Alt-O** to display the **O**ptions menu.

2. Press **T** to choose the Tree List Window command.

   1. Pull down the Options menu.
   2. Choose the Tree List Window command.

See Also *File List Window.* Turns the File List window on and off.

TWO LIST DISPLAY

● **MENU**

| 6.0 | Options➤Modify Display

| 5.5 | Options

● **PURPOSE** Displays the contents of two disks and/or directories. The directory structure is shown in the Tree windows; the files are shown in the File List windows.

To Use Two List Display

Version 6.0

[KEY]

   1. Press **Alt-O** to display the Options menu.
   2. Press **O** to choose the Modify Display command. The Modify Display submenu appears.
   3. Press **W** to choose the Two List Display command.

UNDELETE

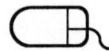

1. Pull down the Options menu, and choose the Modify Display command. The Modify Display submenu appears.

2. Choose the Two List Display command.

Shortcut You can press **Ins** to choose the Two List Display command.

Version 5.5

1. Press **Alt-O** to display the **O**ptions menu.

2. Press **W** to choose the T**w**o List Display command.

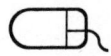

1. Pull down the Options menu.

2. Choose the Two List Display command.

Shortcut You can press **Ins** to choose the Two List Display command.

See Also *One List Display.* Displays one set of Tree/File List windows.

UNDELETE
Version 5.5

See *Undelete Files*.

UNDELETE FILES

• **MENU**

Special

• **PURPOSE** Recovers files that have been accidentally erased. For best results, files should be undeleted as soon as possible after erasure. Otherwise, some or all of the file may be irretrievably lost.

To Recover a Lost File

[KEY]

1. Select the drive and/or the disk that contains the file you want to retrieve.
2. Press **Alt-S** to display the Special menu.
3. Press **U** to choose the Undelete command.
4. Press ↵ to continue file recovery.
5. Press **F** to recover a lost file. Shell will display a list of files that it can recover. The first character of each file name will be missing.
6. Use the cursor keys to select a file you want to undelete, and press **F5** or **G** for **G**o (version 5.5 only).
7. Type the first letter of the file name you want to retrieve.
8. Press **Alt-U** to undelete the file.
9. Press **A** for **A**utomatic file recovery (manual file recovery requires that you piece the file together byte by byte).
10. Shell tells you whether the file recovery was successful. Press ↵ to return to Shell.

112 UNDELETE FILES

1. Select the drive and/or the disk that contains the file you want to retrieve.
2. Pull down the Special menu, and choose the Undelete command.
3. Click on the Continue button.
4. Click on the File button to recover a file. Shell will display a list of files that it can recover. The first character of each file name will be missing.
5. Use the cursor keys to select a file you want to undelete, and press **F5** or **G** for **G**o (version 5.5 only).
6. Type the first letter of the file name you want to retrieve.
7. Press **Alt-U** to undelete the file.
8. Click on the Automatic button to do an automatic file recovery (manual file recovery requires that you piece the file together byte by byte).
9. Shell tells you whether the file recovery was successful. Click on Continue to return to Shell.

• **NOTES** If you are using the PC Tools Mirror program (see Part III) and the Delete Tracking option (MIRROR /T), Shell displays some additional dialog boxes during file recovery. After you choose the Undelete command and indicate that you want to recover a file, Shell asks you whether you want to use the Del Track method or the DOS Dir method. The DOS Dir method is the same as outlined in the steps above; when using the Del Track method, Shell provides the full names of the deleted files. You do not have to provide the first letter of the file name prior to recovery.

UNSELECT FILES

• MENU

6.0 Options➤Modify Display

5.5 Options

• **PURPOSE** Deselects highlighted files in the File List window. (The command is called *Reset Selected Files* in version 5.5.)

To Unselect a File in the File List Window

Version 6.0

[KEY]

1. Press **Alt-O** to display the Options menu.
2. Press **O** to choose the Modify Display command. The Modify Display submenu appears.
3. Press **U** to choose the Unselect Files command.

1. Pull down the Options menu.
2. Choose the Modify Display command. The Modify Display submenu appears.
3. Choose the Unselect Files command.

Shortcut Press the **F4** function key to deselect all files quickly.

Version 5.5

[KEY]

1. Press **Alt-O** to display the Options menu.
2. Press **R** to choose the Reset Selected Files command.

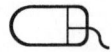

🖱

1. Pull down the Options menu.
2. Choose the Reset Selected Files command.

Shortcut   Press the **F4** function key to deselect all files quickly.

VERIFY
Version 5.5

See *Verify File*.

VERIFY DISK

● **MENU**

Disk

● **PURPOSE**   Verifies the integrity of the currently selected disk. Data errors, if found, are noted by their logical sector number location.

To Verify the Integrity of a Disk

[KEY]

1. Select the disk you want to verify.
2. Press **Alt-D** to display the **D**isk menu.
3. Press **V** to choose the **V**erify Disk command. The Disk Verify dialog box appears.
4. Press **V** to proceed with the verification, or press **C** to cancel (press **X** for Exit if you have version 5.5).
5. You can stop the disk verification at any time by pressing **X** for Exit.

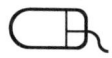

1. Select the disk you want to verify.
2. Pull down the Disk menu, and choose the Verify Disk command. The Disk Verify dialog box appears.
3. Click on the Verify button to proceed with the verification, or click on Cancel (click on Exit if you have version 5.5).
4. You can stop the disk verification at any time by clicking on the Exit button.

See Also   *Verify File*. Verifies the integrity of individual files on your disks. You can also use the *Compress* program and *Diskfix* program (version 6.0 only) to analyze the media surface of your disks.

VERIFY FILE

● **MENU**

File

- **PURPOSE** Verifies the integrity of a file.

To Verify the Integrity of a File

[KEY]

1. Select one or more files you want to verify.
2. Press **Alt-F** to display the File menu.
3. Press **V** to choose the Verify File command (press **Y** for Verify if you are using version 5.5). Shell checks each file in turn, indicating the progress of each file verification.
4. Press **X** for Exit.

1. Click on one or more files you want to verify.
2. Pull down the File menu, and choose the Verify File command. Shell checks each file in turn, indicating the progress of each file verification.
3. Click on the Exit button to return to Shell.

See Also *Verify Disk.* Checks the integrity of the entire disk. You can also use the *Compress* program and *Diskfix* program (version 6.0 only) to check the integrity of the media surface of your disks.

VIEW
Version 5.5

- **MENU**

File

VIEW 117

- **PURPOSE** Displays the contents of the currently selected file. You can view ASCII files, binary files, and document files created by other applications. You can only view the contents of the file; you cannot edit the file. When you view documents created by various applications, such as dBASE or Lotus 1-2-3, Shell presents them properly formatted. Version 5.5 provides only two document *filters*, for dBASE III/IV documents and Lotus 1-2-3 documents.

To View a File

[KEY]

1. Select a file to view.
2. Press **Alt-F** to display the File menu.
3. Press **V** to choose the View command. The View window appears.
4. When you are finished viewing the document, press the **F3** function key to exit the View window.

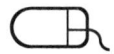

1. Select a file to view.
2. Pull down the File menu, and choose the View command. The View window appears.
3. When you are finished viewing the document, click inside the Close box in the upper-left corner of the View window.

- **NOTES** Press any of the following keys to see more of the document in the View window:

To Move To	Press
Top of document	Home
End of document	End
Down one page	PgDn
Up one page	PgUp

VIEW/EDIT DISK

• MENU

Disk

• **PURPOSE** Displays the sectors of the currently selected disk. The contents of the sectors are displayed in ASCII format and hexadecimal format. You can edit any byte on the disk, if desired (not recommended unless you are restoring a damaged disk).

To Display a Disk's Sectors

KEY

1. Select the disk you want to view or edit.
2. Press **Alt-D** to display the **D**isk menu.
3. Press **E** to choose the View/Edit Disk command. The Disk View window appears, showing you the data placed at the very beginning of the disk (sector 0000000).

You can now move to a different sector, scan sectors, or edit individual bytes, as detailed in the Notes section.

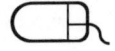

1. Select the disk you want to view or edit.
2. Pull down the Disk menu, and choose the View/Edit Disk command. The Disk View window appears, showing you the data placed at the very beginning of the disk (sector 0000000).

You can now move to a different sector, scan sectors, or edit individual bytes, as detailed in the Notes section.

VIEW/EDIT DISK

- **NOTES** The Disk View window offers the following commands for viewing and editing disks:

Version 6.0

Key	Function
PgDn	Move down one page
PgUp	Move up one page
Home	Move to beginning of disk
End	Move to end of disk
F3	Exit Disk View
F6	Move to new sector
F7	Edit sector
F8	Show directory or file name current sector belongs to (or indicate current sector is boot, root, or FAT data)

Version 5.5

Key	Function
PgDn	Move down one page
PgUp	Move up one page
Home	Move to beginning of disk
End	Move to end of disk
F3	Exit Disk View
S	Move to new sector
E	Edit sector
N	Show directory or file name current sector belongs to (or indicate current sector is boot, root, or FAT data)

Refer to the *Hex Edit File* command for more information on how to edit data within the Disk View window.

See Also *Hex Edit File, Edit File.* These commands enable you to edit individual files.

VIEWER CFG.
Version 6.0 Only

● **MENU**

Options➤Setup Configuration

● **PURPOSE** Alters the arrangement (tiling) of windows when you view a file (the View window must be unzoomed). You have a choice of vertical or horizontal tiling. (*Cfg.* is the abbreviation for *configuration*.)

To Tile Windows

KEY

1. Press **Alt-O** to display the **O**ptions menu.
2. Press **C** to choose the Setup **C**onfiguration command. The Setup Configuration submenu appears. The current setting of the View Cfg. command is shown as VERT (for vertical) or HORZ (for horizontal).
3. Press **V** to choose the **V**iewer Cfg. command. The new setting of the command (either VERT or HORZ) is shown.
4. Press the **F3** function key to exit the menu.

1. Pull down the Options menu, and choose the Setup Configuration command. The Setup Configuration submenu appears. The current setting of the Viewer Cfg. command is shown as VERT (for vertical) or HORZ (for horizontal).

2. Click on the Viewer Cfg. command. The new setting of the command (either VERT or HORZ) is shown.
3. Click anywhere outside the menu to go back to Shell.

• **NOTES**   Text and binary files are generally viewed more easily in the horizontal configuration.

VIEW WINDOW
Version 6.0 Only

• **MENU**

Options

• **PURPOSE**   Turns the View window on and off. The current setting of the window (either ON or OFF) is shown beside the View Window command on the Options menu.

To Turn View Window On or Off

KEY

1. Press **Alt-O** to display the **O**ptions menu.
2. Press **V** to choose the **V**iew Window command.

1. Pull down the Options menu.
2. Choose the View Window command.

WAIT ON DOS SCREEN
Version 6.0 Only

- **MENU**

Options➤Setup Configuration

- **PURPOSE**   When set to ON, temporarily halts the screen display after a DOS command is executed or a program is run from the DOS prompt. Shell is reactivated only after you press a key. When set to OFF, Shell restarts immediately after the DOS command is completed.

To Use Wait on DOS Screen

[KEY]

1. Press **Alt-O** to display the **O**ptions menu.
2. Press **C** to choose the Setup **C**onfiguration command. The Setup Configuration submenu appears. The current setting of the Wait on DOS Screen command is shown as ON or OFF.
3. Press **W** to choose the **W**ait on DOS Screen command. The new setting of the command (either ON or OFF) is shown.
4. Press the **F3** function key to exit the menu.

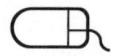

1. Pull down the Options menu, and choose the Setup Configuration command. The Setup Configuration submenu appears. The current setting of the Wait on DOS Screen command is shown as ON or OFF.
2. Click on the Wait on DOS Screen command. The new setting of the command (either ON or OFF) is shown.

ZOOM THE CURRENT WINDOW
Version 6.0 Only

3. Click anywhere outside the menu to go back to Shell.

- **MENU**

Options

- **PURPOSE** Zooms the currently selected window in or out. When zoomed out, the window is full-screen. When zoomed in, the window returns to its default size.

To Zoom a Window

[KEY]

1. Select the window you want to zoom.
2. Press **Alt-O** to display the Options menu.
3. Press **Z** to choose the Zoom the Current Window command.

1. Click on the window you want to zoom.
2. Pull down the Options menu, and choose the Zoom the Current Window command.

Shortcut Press **F8** to zoom the current window in or out.

Part Two

DESKTOP

The Desktop program combines a bevy of handy "mini-applications" in one convenient, easy-to-use module. You merely select the application you want from a menu. By loading it as memory-resident, you can use Desktop to augment the programs you already use or in place of more complex stand-alone programs.

Desktop contains the following applications:

- Word processor
- Outliner
- Data manager
- Communications terminal
- Fax terminal (version 6.0 only)
- Appointment scheduler
- Multifunction calculators
- Macro command editor
- Clipboard
- Utilities

STARTING DESKTOP

Desktop must be loaded before you can use its applications. You can load Desktop as a stand-alone application or as a RAM-resident application. When it is RAM-resident, you can activate it while using DOS or another program by pressing the appropriate hotkey.

To Load Desktop as a Stand-Alone Application

1. At the DOS prompt, type **DESKTOP**.
2. Press ↵.

To Load Desktop as a RAM-Resident Application

1. At the DOS prompt, type **DESKTOP /R**.
2. Press ↵.

To Activate Desktop While RAM-Resident

- Press **Ctrl-spacebar**.

Pressing **Ctrl-spacebar** while in Desktop returns you to DOS or the original application you were in.

To Remove Desktop from Memory after Loading as RAM-Resident

1. At the DOS prompt, type **KILL**.
2. Press ↵.

NOTEPADS

- **PURPOSE** A fully functional word processor with writing, editing, formatting, and printing functions. Notepads works with ASCII or WordStar files.

To Open Notepads

[KEY]

1. Press **Alt-D** to display the **D**esktop menu (if it isn't already displayed).
2. Press **N** to choose the **N**otepads command. The Notepads file box appears.

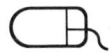

[mouse]

1. Pull down the Desktop menu.
2. Choose the Notepads command. The Notepads file box appears.

To Edit an Existing File

[KEY]

1. Press **Tab** to move the highlight to the file list.
2. In the Notepads file box, press the cursor keys to highlight the file you want to edit.
3. Press **Alt-L** to load the file. The file is opened and displayed on the Notepads editing screen.

1. In the Notepads file box, scroll through the list to highlight the file you want.
2. Click on the Load button. The file is opened and displayed on the Notepads editing screen.

If you know the name of the file you want to open, type it at the file-name field, and press ↵. Include a drive and full path, if desired.

Notepads initially sets the default file extension to .TXT. Only those files with the .TXT extension, as well as available directories and disk drives, are displayed in the file list. If the file you want to open has a different extension, edit the command line as desired. (The file list initially shows only drive letters if there are not yet any saved files.)

To look at the files on a different disk, highlight the appropriate drive, such as [-A-] for drive A.

To Create a New File

1. Press **Alt-N** to start a new file.
2. If the WORK.TXT default document already exists, press ↵ to start a new document, or press **C** (for **C**ancel) to go back to the Notepads file box.

1. Click on the New button.
2. If the WORK.TXT default document already exists, click on the OK button to start a new document, or click on the Cancel button to go back to the Notepads file box.

To Write and Edit with Notepads

Notepads works like most word processors. Table 2.1 describes the keys you can use to write and edit text in Notepads.

To Load an Existing Document

KEY

1. Press **Alt-F** to display the File menu.
2. Press **L** to choose the Load command. The Notepads file box appears.

Table 2.1: Key Functions in Notepads

KEY	FUNCTION
Tab	Insert tab at cursor
↵	Start new line
Backspace	Erase character to left of cursor
Del	Erase character under cursor
Ins	Turn Typeover on or off
Home	Move to beginning of current line
End	Move to end of current line
→	Move right one character
←	Move left one character
↑	Move up one line
↓	Move down one line
Ctrl-→	Move right one word
Ctrl-←	Move left one word
PgUp	Scroll up one window
PgDn	Scroll down one window
Ctrl-PgUp	Scroll text up one line
Ctrl-PgDn	Scroll text down one line
Home, Home	Move to top line of window
End, End	Move to bottom line of window
Ctrl-Home	Move to top of document
Ctrl-End	Move to bottom of document

130 NOTEPADS

3. Select the file you want to load.

Shortcut   Press **F4** to choose the Load command.

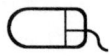

1. Pull down the File menu, and choose the Load command. The Notepads file box appears.

2. Click on the file you want to load.

If you are currently working on a document, save it first before loading a new one. If you want to combine the text of another document with the current document, use the Insert File command.

To Save a Document

1. Press **Alt-F** to display the File menu.

2. Press **S** to choose the Save command.

3. Press **Tab** to select one of the following options:
- PC Tools Desktop: saves the file in default Desktop format.
- ASCII: saves the file in straight ASCII format.
- Make Backup File: creates a backup file.

4. Press **Alt-S** to initiate the saving of the file.

Shortcut   Press **F5** to save the file.

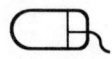

1. Pull down the File menu, and choose the Save command.

2. Click on one of the following options:
- PC Tools Desktop: saves the file in default Desktop format.
- ASCII: saves the file in straight ASCII format.
- Make Backup File: creates a backup file.

3. Click on the Save button to save the file.

You can have Desktop automatically save the file every few minutes by using the Autosave feature (this feature is not a substitute for saving the document manually when you are finished writing and editing).

To use Autosave, follow these steps:

1. Pull down the File menu, and choose the Autosave command.

2. Indicate the time in minutes between each autosave (the default is 5 minutes).

3. Turn Autosave ON (ON is the default).

You can turn off Autosave at any time.

To Print a Notepads File

[KEY]

1. Press **Alt-F** to display the File menu.

2. Press **P** to choose the Print command. The Print dialog box appears.

3. Review the print settings, and make changes as desired.

4. Press **Alt-P** to start printing.

1. Pull down the File menu, and choose the Print command. The Print dialog box appears.

2. Review the print settings, and make changes as desired.

3. Click on the Print button to start printing.

In the Print dialog box, you have your choice of printing one or more copies of the file and of printing to any of six destinations.

- The default number of copies is 1. If you want additional copies, press **Tab** until the Copies field is highlighted, and type a new number. Press ↵.
- The print destination is the computer port that your printer is connected to. Normally, this is LPT1 for a parallel printer, but you can change it to LPT2, LPT3, COM1, COM2, or Disk File. To change the port, press **Tab** to move the highlight to the port options area, then press ↑ and ↓ to select a port. The LPT ports are parallel connections; the COM ports are serial connections. The Disk File option enables you to save the formatted document in a disk file.

To Exit the Notepads Editor without Saving

KEY

1. Press **Alt-F** to display the File menu.
2. Press **X** to choose the Exit Without Saving command.

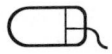

1. Pull down the File Menu.
2. Choose the Exit Without Saving command.

Shortcut Press **F3** to leave the Notepads editor without saving the document.

To Cut, Copy, and Paste Text

KEY

1. Move the cursor to the start of the text you want to cut or copy.
2. Press **Alt-E** to display the Edit menu.
3. Press **M** to choose the Mark Block command.

NOTEPADS 133

4. Move the cursor to the end of the text you want to cut or copy. The selected text is highlighted.
5. Press **Alt-E** to display the Edit menu.
6. Press **T** for **C**u**t** to move the text to the clipboard, or press **C** for **C**opy to copy the text to the clipboard.
7. Move the cursor to where you want to place the text.
8. Press **Alt-E** to display the Edit menu.
9. Press **P** for **P**aste from Clipboard to paste the text into the document.

1. Drag over the text you want to cut or copy.
2. Pull down the Edit menu, and choose the Cut to Clipboard or Copy to Clipboard command.
3. Click on the area where you want to place the text.
4. Pull down the Edit menu, and choose the Paste from Clipboard command.

To Delete All Text in the Document

[KEY]

1. Press **Alt-E** to display the Edit menu.
2. Press **D** to choose the **D**elete All Text command.
3. Verify that you want to delete all the text in the document by pressing the ↵ key, or press **C** for **C**ancel.

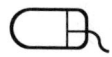

1. Pull down the Edit menu, and choose the Delete All Text command.
2. Click on the OK button to verify the command, or click on Cancel.

To Insert a File in the Current Document

KEY

1. Press **Alt-E** to display the Edit menu.
2. Press **I** to choose the Insert File command.
3. Select the file to insert from the Notepads file list.

1. Pull down the Edit menu, and choose the Insert File command.
2. Select the file to insert from the Notepads file list.

To Go to a Specific Line in the Document

KEY

1. Press **Alt-E** to display the Edit menu.
2. Press **G** to choose the Goto command.
3. Type the line you want to go to, and press ↵. Press ↵ a second time to confirm, or simply press **Alt-O** after typing the line number.

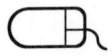

1. Pull down the Edit menu, and choose the Goto command.
2. Type the line you want to go to, and click on OK.

To Check Spelling in Your Document

KEY

1. Press **Alt-E** to display the Edit menu.

2. Press one of the following keys:
   - **W** to spell-check current word
   - **S** to spell-check the text on the current screen
   - **F** to spell-check all the text in the file
3. During the spell-check, press any of the following keys:
   - **I** to ignore the selected word
   - **C** to correct the selected word (provide new spelling)
   - **A** to add the word to the user dictionary
   - **Q** to quit spell-checking

1. Pull down the Edit menu, and click on one of the following:
   - *Spellcheck Word* to spell-check the current word
   - *Spellcheck Screen* to spell-check the text on the current screen
   - *Spellcheck File* to spell-check all the text in the file
2. During the spell-check, click on any of the following:
   - *Ignore* to skip the selected word
   - *Correct* to correct the selected word (provide new spelling)
   - *Add* to add the word to the user dictionary
   - *Quit* to stop spell-checking

Shortcut Press **F7** to start a spell-check of the entire file.

To Find Text within a Document

1. Press **Alt-S** to display the Search menu.
2. Press **F** to choose the Find command.
3. Type the text you want to search for in the entry blank.

4. If desired, use the **Tab** key to highlight the Case Sensitive and Whole Words Only options, and press ↵ to select them.

5. Press **Alt-F** to choose the Find Next command, or press **Alt-C** for Cancel.

Repeat step 5 for each occurrence of the word.

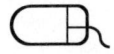

1. Pull down the Search menu, and choose the Find command.

2. Type the text you want to search for in the entry blank.

3. If desired, click on the Case Sensitive and Whole Words Only options.

4. Click on the Find Next button to find the next occurrence of the word, or click on the Cancel button.

Repeat step 4 for each occurrence of the word.

To Find and Replace Text within a Document

1. Press **Alt-S** to display the Search menu.

2. Press **R** to choose the Replace command.

3. If the Search For entry field isn't selected, press the **Tab** key until it is.

4. Type the text you want to find in the entry blank. Press **Tab**.

5. Type the replacement text in the Replace With entry blank. Press **Tab**.

6. Use the cursor keys and ↵ to select one of the following options:
- Replace one time
- Replace all
- Verify before replace

NOTEPADS 137

7. If desired, use the **Tab** key to highlight the Case Sensitive and Whole Words Only options, and press ↵ to select them.

8. Press one of the following:
- **Alt-F** to find the next occurrence of the search word
- **Alt-R** to replace the word
- **Alt-C** to cancel

Repeat step 8 for each occurrence of the word.

1. Pull down the Search menu, and choose the Replace command.

2. Click on the Search For entry blank, and type the text you want to find.

3. Click on the Replace With entry blank, and type the replacement text.

4. Click on one of the following options:
- Replace one time
- Replace all
- Verify before replace

5. If desired, click on the Case Sensitive and Whole Words Only options.

6. Click on one of the following:
- *Find* to search for the next occurrence of the search word
- *Replace* to replace the word
- *Cancel* to leave the Search function

Repeat step 6 for each occurrence of the word.

To Change the Page Layout

[KEY]

1. Press **Alt-C** to display the Controls menu.
2. Press **P** to choose the Page Layout command.
3. Enter settings for margins, paper size, line spacing, and starting page number (press the **Tab** key to move between the entry blanks).
4. Press ↵ or **Alt-O** to accept the new settings, or press **Alt-C** to cancel.

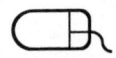

1. Pull down the Controls menu, and choose the Page Layout command.
2. Enter settings for margins, paper size, line spacing, and starting page number.
3. Click on the OK button to accept the new settings, or click on the Cancel button.

Every new Notepads document uses the following format defaults:

Setting	Default
Left margin	8
Right margin	73
Top margin	6
Bottom margin	6
Paper size	66
Line spacing	1
Starting page #	1

To Add a Repeating Header or Footer

[KEY]

1. Press **Alt-C** to display the Controls menu.
2. Press **H** to choose the Header/Footer command.
3. Type the text for the header, or press **Tab** and type the text for the footer.
4. Press ↵ or **Alt-O** to accept the header and/or footer, or press **Alt-C** to cancel.

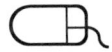

1. Pull down the Controls menu, and choose the Header/Footer command.
2. Type the text for the header, or press **Tab** and type the text for the footer.
3. Click on the OK button to accept the header and/or footer, or click on the Cancel button.

To Set the Tab Ruler

[KEY]

1. Press **Alt-C** to display the Controls menu.
2. Press **E** to choose the Tab Ruler Edit command.
3. To set a new tab stop, use the cursor keys to position the cursor on the ruler, and press **Ins**. To delete an existing tab stop, use the cursor keys to position the cursor on the ruler, and press **Del**.
4. Press **Esc** when you're finished.

🖱

1. Pull down the Controls menu, and choose the Tab Ruler Edit command.
2. To set a new tab stop, use the cursor keys to position the cursor on the ruler, and press **Ins**. To delete an existing tab stop, use the cursor keys to position the cursor on the ruler, and press **Del**.
3. Press **Esc** when you're finished.

To Save the Current Document Setup

[KEY]

1. Press **Alt-C** to display the Controls menu.
2. Press **S** to choose the Save Setup command.

🖱

1. Pull down the Controls menu.
2. Choose the Save Setup command.

To Set the Document Display

[KEY]

1. Press **Alt-C** to display the Controls menu.
2. Press one of the following keys (a check mark beside the command tells you the option is turned on):
   - **T** to turn **T**ab Ruler Display on and off
   - **O** to turn **O**vertype mode on and off
   - **C** to turn **C**ontrol Character Display on and off
   - **W** to turn **W**ordwrap on and off
   - **A** to turn **A**uto Indent on and off

1. Pull down the Controls menu.
2. Click on one of the following to turn the corresponding option on or off (a check mark beside the command tells you the option is turned on):
   - Tab Ruler Display
   - Overtype mode
   - Control Character Display
   - Wordwrap
   - Auto Indent

You can also use the commands on the Window menu to set the document display:

- The *Change Colors* command changes the colors of the screen.
- The *Video Size* command (version 6.0 only) changes the number of rows displayed.
- The *Move* command moves the window.
- The *Resize* command resizes the window.
- The *Zoom* command zooms the window in or out.

OUTLINES

- **PURPOSE** Uses most of the same text-writing, editing, and formatting commands as Notepads, but adds specialized commands for creating documents in standard outline format. An additional menu, titled Headlines, controls the appearance and position of outline text.

- **NOTES** Follow the same procedures detailed in the Using Notepads section of this chapter to start outlines, open existing outline documents, create new documents, etc.

To access any of the Headlines commands, press **Alt-H** to display the Headlines menu. Here are the commands on the Headlines menu (the *current headline* is the headline containing the cursor):

Command	Function
Expand **C**urrent	Expands all headlines below current headline
Expand **A**ll	Expands all collapsed headings
Show Levels	Displays headlines up to level you indicate
Collapse Current	Collapses all levels following current one
Main Headline Only	Collapses all levels except for main headline
Promote	Moves headline to next higher level
Demote	Moves headline to next lower level

DATABASES

- **PURPOSE** Databases is a dBASE-file-compatible data management program. With it, you can enter, organize, and store information for later recall. Coupled with Notepads, you can merge data with documents to create form letters.

Keep the following points in mind when using Databases:

- Each database file can contain up to 10,000 records (3500 in version 5.5).
- Each record can contain up to 4000 characters.
- Each record can be divided into as many as 128 fields.
- Each field can contain up to 70 characters.
- Database files are given .DBF file extensions and are compatible with dBASE III.

DATABASES 143

- Record files, with .REC extensions, are used exclusively by Databases.
- Form files, with .FOR extensions, are Notepads word processing files.
- Databases ignores the Memo field in dBASE documents.
- Computed fields from dBASE files are ignored in Databases.
- Databases automatically saves your changes when you exit the current database or leave Desktop.

To Open Databases

[KEY]

1. Press **Alt-D** to display the **D**esktop menu (if it isn't already displayed).
2. Press **D** to choose the **D**atabases command. The Databases file box appears.

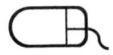

1. Pull down the Desktop menu.
2. Choose the Databases command. The Databases file box appears.

To Edit an Existing File

[KEY]

1. Press **Tab** to move the highlight to the file list.
2. In the Databases dialog box, press the cursor keys to highlight the file you want to edit.
3. Press **Alt-L** to load the file. The file is opened and displayed on the Databases editing screen.

144 DATABASES

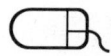

🖱

1. In the Databases file box, scroll through the list to highlight the file you want to edit.
2. Click on the Load button. The file is opened and displayed on the Databases editing screen.

If you know the name of the file you want to open, type it at the file-name field, and press ↵. Include a drive and full path, if desired.

Databases initially sets the default file extension to .DBF. Only those files with the .DBF extension, as well as available directories and disk drives, are displayed in the file list. If the file you want to open has a different extension, edit the command line as desired.

To look at the files on a different disk, highlight the appropriate drive, such as [-A-] for drive A.

To Create a New Databases File

[KEY]

1. Press **Alt-N** to start a new file.
2. If the WORK.DBF default document already exists, press ↵ to start a new document, or press **C** (for **C**ancel) to go back to the Databases file box.
3. Complete the database form as detailed below.

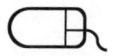

🖱

1. Click on the New button.
2. If the WORK.DBF default document already exists, click on the OK button to start a new document, or click on the Cancel button to go back to the Databases file box.
3. Complete the database form as detailed below.

When creating a new database, you have to indicate the number and variety of fields it will contain. Complete the database by filling in the Field Editor box. As you fill in the box, press **Tab** to move to the next entry blank.

- Type the name of the field (such as *Name, Telephone Number,* or *ZIP Code*) in the Field Name entry box, then press **Tab** or ↵. For maximum compatibility with other database programs, do not use spaces in field names.

- For the Field type, use the cursor keys to indicate Character, Numeric, Logical, or Date, and press ↵.

- Type the maximum number of characters that the field will accept in the Size entry box. The default is 1. For example, if you want to enter five-digit ZIP codes, enter 5 as the field size. The size of a Logical field—which is used to enter True/False responses (T, t, F, or f)—should be kept at 1.

- Type the number of decimal places you want displayed in the field when entering numbers. The default is 0.

When you are finished entering the field data, do one of the following:

- To accept the field, press **Alt-A**, or click on the Add button. You can now create another field.

- To ignore the new field, press **Alt-C**, or click on the Cancel button.

- To review the next field or previous field (to make changes to them), press **Alt-N** or **Alt-P**, as desired (or click on Next or Previous).

- To delete the current field, press **Alt-D**, or click on the Delete button.

- To save the field definitions, press **Alt-S**, or click on the Save button.

To Write and Edit with Databases

Table 2.2 describes the keys you can use to write and edit with Databases.

146 DATABASES

Table 2.2: Key Functions in Databases

KEY	FUNCTION
Tab	Move to next field
Shift-Tab	Move to previous field
↵	Accept text and move to next field
Backspace	Erase character to left of cursor
Del	Erase character under cursor
Ins	Turn Typeover on or off
→	Move right one character
←	Move left one character
↑	Move up one line
↓	Move down one line
PgUp	Scroll up one window
PgDn	Scroll down one window
F4	Go to first record in database
F5	Go to previous record
F6	Go to next record
F7	Search for record/text
F8	Add new record

To Load an Existing Form

KEY

1. Press **Alt-F** to display the File menu.
2. Press **L** to choose the Load Form command. The Databases file box appears.
3. Select the file you want to load.

DATABASES

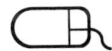

1. Pull down the File menu, and choose the Load Form command. The Databases file box appears.
2. Click on the file you want to load.

To Print a Database

1. Press **Alt-F** to display the File menu.
2. Press **P** to choose the Print command.
3. Use the cursor keys to select one of the following options (in version 6.0, you must select a printer port first):
   - Print selected records
   - Print current record
   - Print field names
4. Press **P** to print or **C** to cancel.
5. Select the desired print options (see "To Print a Notepads File").
6. Press **Alt-P** to start printing.

1. Pull down the File menu, and choose the Print command.
2. Click on one of the following options (in version 6.0, you must select a printer port first):
   - Print selected records
   - Print current record
   - Print field names
3. Click on the Print button or Cancel button.

148 DATABASES

   4. Select the desired print options (see "To Print a Notepads File").
   5. Click on the Print button to start printing.

To Add a New Record

[KEY]

   1. Press **Alt-E** to display the Edit menu.
   2. Press **A** to choose the Add New Record command.
   3. Enter the data for the record.

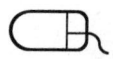

   1. Pull down the Edit menu, and choose the Add New Record command.
   2. Enter the data for the record.

Shortcut   Press **F8** to choose the Add New Record command.

To Delete a Record

[KEY]

   1. Select the record you want to delete.
   2. Press **Alt-E** to display the Edit menu.
   3. Press **D** to choose the Delete Record command.

   1. Select the record you want to delete.
   2. Pull down the Edit menu, and choose the Delete New Record command.

To Select Records

KEY

1. Press **Alt-E** to display the Edit menu.
2. Press either of the following keys:
   - **L** to choose the Select All Records command. All records in the database are selected automatically.
   - **R** to choose the Select Records command. You can now indicate those fields you want to use as search criteria.

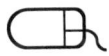

1. Pull down the Edit menu.
2. Choose either of the following commands:
   - Select All Records: to select all records in the database.
   - Select Records: to indicate those fields you want to use as search criteria.

When using the Select Records command, you can enter up to eight search criteria. Choosing the Select Records command displays the Select Records dialog box, which consists of two columns, labeled Field Name and Field Criteria.

- In the Field Name column, enter the name of the field that contains the data you are looking for.
- In the Field Criteria column, enter the specific information you want to find.

If you want to find a range of records, enter the start and stop range and separate them with two dots. For instance, to display all records in which the Age field is between 18 and 24, enter **18..24** in the Field Criteria column.

To Sort the Database

[KEY]

1. Press **Alt-E** to choose the Edit command.
2. Press **S** to choose the Sort Database command. The Sort Database dialog box appears.
3. Press **N** or **P** (for Next and Previous) to sift through the field names until you find the one you want to sort by (such as *Name, City,* or *ZIP*).
4. Press **S** to start the sort, or press **C** to cancel.

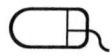

1. Pull down the Edit menu, and choose the Sort Database command. The Sort Database dialog box appears.
2. Click on the Next or Previous button to sift through the field names until you find the one you want to sort by (such as *Name, City,* or *ZIP*).
3. Click on the Sort button to start the sort, or click on the Cancel button.

To Search for Text within a Database

[KEY]

1. Press **Alt-S** to display the Search menu.
2. Press **F** to choose the Find Text in All Fields command. The Search All Fields dialog box appears.
3. Type the search string you want to look for in the Search Data entry field.
4. Press the **Tab** key to move the highlight to the options area.

DATABASES 151

5. Use the cursor keys to choose one of the following options:
   - Search all records
   - Search selected records
   - Search from current record
6. Press **S** to start the search, or press **C** to cancel.

🖱️

1. Pull down the Search menu, and choose the Find Text in All Fields command. The Search All Fields dialog box appears.
2. Type the search string you want to look for in the Search Data entry field.
3. Click on one of the following options:
   - Search all records
   - Search selected records
   - Search from current record
4. Click on the Search button to start the search, or click on the Cancel button.

To Go to a Specific Record

[KEY]

1. Press **Alt-S** to display the Search menu.
2. Press **G** to choose the Goto Record command.
3. Type the number of the record you want to go to.
4. Press **Alt-G** to go to the record, or press **Alt-C** to cancel.

🖱️

1. Pull down the Search menu, and choose the Goto Record command.
2. Type the number of the record you want to go to.
3. Click on the Goto button, or click on the Cancel button.

To Change Page Layout

Follow the steps outlined in the Notepads section for changing page layout. Databases uses the same defaults.

MODEM TELECOMMUNICATIONS

- **PURPOSE** The Modem Telecommunications terminal allows you to connect to a distant computer via the phone lines. The Modem Telecommunications module stores often-used phone numbers and communications parameters so that you can select a number and dial it instantly.

Before you can use the module, you must enter a phone number and other settings in the Telecommunications window.

To Open Modem Telecommunications

[KEY]

1. Press **Alt-D** to display the Desktop menu (if it isn't already displayed).
2. Press **T** to choose the Telecommunications command. (If you have version 6.0, press **T**, then press **M** for Modem Telecommunications.) The Telecommunications window appears.

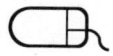

1. Pull down the Desktop menu.
2. Choose the Telecommunications command. (If you have version 6.0, choose Telecommunications, then the Modem

MODEM TELECOMMUNICATIONS

Telecommunications command.) The Telecommunications window appears.

To Enter a Communications Setting

[KEY]

1. Press **Alt-E** to display the Edit menu.
2. Press **C** to choose the Create New Entry command. The Edit Phone Directory window appears.

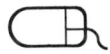

🖱️

1. Pull down the Edit menu.
2. Choose the Create New Entry command. The Edit Phone Directory window appears.

Enter the desired data in the Phone Directory window:

- Name (for reference purposes)
- Phone number to dial
- Script file to use
- User ID (version 6.0 only)
- Field 1, Field 2
- Password (version 6.0 only)
- Database to use (version 6.0 only)
- Terminal type
- Port (version 5.5 only; in version 6.0, set the port by using the Modem Setup command on the Setup menu)
- Communications parameters: parity, data bits, stop bits, baud rate, duplex
- Dial type: pulse or tone (accessed as Port is)
- File filters: line feeds, carriage returns
- Flow control

Press **Alt-A** to accept the settings, or press **Alt-C** to cancel the settings.

You can edit the settings at any time by highlighting the Edit entry in the Telecommunications window and choosing the Edit Entry command on the Edit menu.

To Place a Call

[KEY]

1. Use the cursor keys to select the entry you want in the Telecommunications window.
2. Press ↵ to initiate the call. Desktop dials the number.

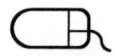

- Double-click on the entry you want to dial. Desktop dials the number.

To Hang Up the Phone

[KEY]

1. Press **Alt-A** to display the Actions menu.
2. Press **H** to choose the Hangup Phone command.

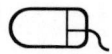

1. Pull down the Actions menu.
2. Choose the Hangup Phone command.

To Send a File

The following procedures assume that an online connection has been established.

MODEM TELECOMMUNICATIONS

KEY

1. Press **Alt-S** to display the Send menu (this menu only appears when your computer is online).
2. Press **A** to send an ASCII file, or press **X** to send an XMODEM file.
3. Use the cursor keys to select the file you want to send.
4. Press **L** to select Load.

1. Pull down the Send menu (this menu only appears when your computer is online), and choose the ASCII or XMODEM command to send an ASCII or XMODEM file.
2. Double-click on the file you want to send. Select Load.

To Receive a File

The following procedures assume that an online connection has been established.

KEY

1. Press **Alt-R** to display the Receive menu (this menu only appears when your computer is online).
2. Press **A** to receive an ASCII file, or press **X** to receive an XMODEM file.
3. Type a name for the file.
4. Press ↵.

1. Pull down the Receive menu (this menu only appears when your computer is online), and choose the ASCII or XMODEM command to receive an ASCII or XMODEM file.

156 FAX TELECOMMUNICATIONS

2. Type a name for the file.
3. Press ↵ or select Save.

After receiving an ASCII file, choose the End Transfer command on the Actions menu. You can also use this command to abort a file transfer or reception at any time.

FAX TELECOMMUNICATIONS
Version 6.0 Only

● **PURPOSE** Enables you to use your PC as a facsimile machine for sending and receiving faxes. Your computer must be equipped with a compatible fax board.

To Open Fax Telecommunications

[KEY]

1. Press **Alt-D** to display the Desktop menu (if it isn't already displayed).
2. Press **T** to choose the Telecommunications command.
3. Press **S** to choose the Send a Fax command. The Send Fax Directory window appears.

1. Pull down the Desktop menu, and choose the Telecommunications command.
2. Choose the Send a Fax command. The Send Fax Directory window appears.

To Send a Fax Entry

[KEY]

1. Press **Alt-A** to display the Actions menu.
2. Press **A** to choose the Add a New Entry command.
3. In the appropriate entry fields, type the following:
   - Who you're sending the fax to, who it's from, and date and time
   - The fax phone number to dial
   - Comments (if desired)
   - Transmission resolution (fine, normal, or fax board to fax board)
4. Press **Alt-S** for Select Files and Send to select an existing file and send it, or press **Alt-C** for Create a New File and Send to create a new file (in a blank Notepads window) and send it.

1. Pull down the Actions menu, and and choose the Add a New Entry command.
2. In the appropriate entry fields, type the following:
   - Who you're sending the fax to, who it's from, and date and time
   - The fax phone number to dial
   - Comments (if desired)
   - Transmission resolution (fine, normal, or fax board to fax board)
3. Click on the Select Files and Send command to select an existing file and send it, or click on the Create a New File and Send command to create a new file (in a blank Notepads window) and send it.

- **NOTES** Once you've created an entry, you can use it later—just select the entry in the Send Fax Directory window and press ↵.

APPOINTMENT SCHEDULER

You can edit the settings at any time by highlighting the entry in the Fax Telecommunications window and choosing the Edit the Current Entry command on the Actions menu.

- **PURPOSE**   Enables you to keep track of important dates and engagements and create quick-reference to-do lists to remind you of important tasks.

To Open the Appointment Scheduler

[KEY]

1. Press **Alt-D** to display the **D**esktop menu (if it isn't already displayed).
2. Press **A** to choose the **A**ppointment Scheduler command. The Appointment Schedule window appears.
3. Select the .TM Appointment Scheduler file you want to use, or press **Alt-N** to create a new file.

1. Pull down the Desktop menu, and choose the Appointment Scheduler command. The Appointment Schedule window appears.
2. Double-click on the .TM Appointment Scheduler file you want to use, or click on the New button to create a new file.

The Appointment Schedule window is composed of three smaller windows: a monthly calendar, a to-do list, and a daily diary. Initially, the daily diary window is active; you can activate another window by

To Enter an Appointment for the Day

[KEY]

1. Make sure the Daily Scheduler window is active (press **Tab** until it is).
2. Use the cursor keys to highlight a time of day for the appointment.
3. Press ↵. The Make Appointment window opens.
4. Provide the following information in the window (press **Tab** to switch to each option in turn):
   - Description of the appointment
   - Type of appointment
   - Frequency of the appointment, such as *Today only*, *Every day*, or *Weekly*
   - Duration of the appointment in days, hours, and minutes
   - Type of alarm, if any, for the appointment
5. Press **Alt-M** to make the appointment, or press **Alt-C** to cancel.

1. Make sure the Daily Scheduler window is active (click inside it if it's not).
2. Click on a time of day for the appointment.
3. Press ↵. The Make Appointment window opens.
4. Provide the following information in the window (press **Tab** to switch to each option in turn):
   - Description of the appointment
   - Type of appointment

160 APPOINTMENT SCHEDULER

- Frequency of the appointment, such as *Today only*, *Every day*, or *Weekly*
- Duration of the appointment in days, hours, and minutes
- Type of alarm, if any, for the appointment

5. Click on the Make button to accept the information, or click on the Cancel button.

Initially, the Appointment Scheduler starts its day at 8:00 a.m. and ends at 5:00 p.m., with 15-minute increments. You can select your own start and stop times for your workday; you can also choose 30-minute appointment intervals by using the Appointment Settings command on the Controls menu.

To Enter a To-Do Note

[KEY]

1. Make sure the To-Do List window is active (press **Tab** until it is).
2. Type a note.
3. Press ↵ to accept the note.

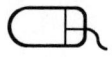

1. Click inside the To-Do List window to make it active.
2. Type a note.
3. Press ↵ to accept the note.

To Change the Displayed Date

[KEY]

1. Make sure the Monthly Calendar window is active (press **Tab** until it is).

2. Use the cursor keys to select a different day of the month. Press **PgUp** and **PgDn** to change months. The current month and year are shown at the top of the calendar.

1. Make sure the Monthly Calendar window is active (click inside it if it's not).
2. Use the cursor keys to select a different day of the month. Press **PgUp** and **PgDn** to change months. The current month and year are shown at the top of the calendar.

CALCULATORS

- **PURPOSE** Desktop provides four types of pop-up calculators:
  - **Algebraic Calculator**: for routine arithmetic
  - **Financial Calculator**: for figuring out financial matters, such as computing present value, future value, and bonds
  - **Programmer's Calculator**: for converting between hexadecimal, octal, binary, and decimal notation
  - **Scientific Calculator**: for solving trigonometric and other scientific equations

To Open a Calculator

1. Press **Alt-D** to display the Desktop menu (if it isn't already displayed).
2. Press **C** to choose the Calculators command.

3. Press one of the following keys:
- **A** to select the **A**lgebraic calculator
- **F** to select the **F**inancial calculator
- **P** to select the **P**rogrammer's (hex) calculator
- **S** to select the **S**cientific calculator

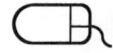

1. Pull down the Desktop menu (if it isn't already displayed), and choose the Calculators command.

2. Click on one of the following:
- Algebraic calculator
- Financial calculator
- Programmer's (hex) calculator
- Scientific calculator

• **NOTES** You can use the keys on the keyboard and numeric keypad to enter digits into the calculators.

MACRO EDITOR

• **PURPOSE** Keyboard macros are shortcuts you can program into Desktop for automating tasks, such as calling a distant computer by using the Modem Telecommunications module, sending a certain file, and logging off. Macros use a special command syntax to duplicate keystrokes.

The Macro Editor window functions the same way as the Notepads window.

CLIPBOARD

- **PURPOSE** Stores text cut or copied from a Desktop accessory or a DOS application. For best results, load Desktop as memory-resident when using the Clipboard command with a DOS application.

To Use the Clipboard

1. Choose the Clipboard command on the Desktop menu. The Clipboard window appears.

2. Choose the Copy to Clipboard command on the Copy/Paste menu.

3. With the keyboard or mouse, select the text you want to copy.

4. Move the cursor where you want to paste the text (or start another application).

5. Choose the Clipboard command on the Desktop menu. The Clipboard window appears.

6. Choose the Paste from Clipboard command on the Copy/Paste menu.

Part Three

THE FILE AND DISK UTILITIES

The PC Tools Deluxe package contains a number of stand-alone utility programs for file management, hard-disk management and backup, and file recovery.

- *PC Backup* archives your hard disk.
- *Compress* defragments files on a hard disk.
- *PC Format* replaces the DOS FORMAT command for safer disk formatting.
- *PC-Cache* uses some of the memory in your computer to hold often-used disk data.
- *Mirror* takes a "snapshot" of critical file areas on a hard disk for faster and more reliable data recovery.
- *Rebuild* reconstructs a hard disk by using information Mirror supplies.
- *Diskfix* repairs damaged disks and recovers lost data.
- *PC Secure* encrypts and decrypts files.

PC BACKUP

• **PURPOSE** PC Backup is a hard-disk archival program. It is used to back up a hard drive on floppy disks or to a streaming tape drive. In case of media failure, the archived data can be used to restore the hard disk. PC Backup allows you to back up and restore the entire contents of a hard-disk drive or selected files only.

To Start PC Backup

1. At the DOS prompt, type **PCBACKUP**.
2. Press ↵.

To Back Up All Files

KEY

1. Press **Alt-B** to display the Backup menu.
2. Press **S** to choose the Start Backup command.
3. Insert disks in the disk drive as instructed by the program.
4. You can stop the backup process at any time by pressing **F3**.

Shortcut Press **F5** to start the backup process.

1. Pull down the Backup menu, and choose the Start Backup command.
2. Insert disks in the disk drive as instructed by the program.
3. You can stop the backup process at any time by pressing **F3**.

To Select/Deselect Files for Backup

KEY

1. Press **Alt-B** to display the **B**ackup directory.
2. Press **H** to select the C**h**oose Directories command.
3. In the Tree window, use the cursor keys to highlight those directories that contain files you don't want to back up.
4. Press ↵ to deselect the directory, or press **Tab** to move the cursor to the file list, use the cursor keys to highlight a file, and press ↵ to deselect the single file.

Repeat steps 3 and 4 for each directory or file you want to deselect. Files are reselected in the same manner.

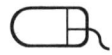

1. Access the Backup directory, and select the Choose Directories command.
2. In the Tree window, click on those directories that contain files you don't want to back up, or use the mouse to select a directory, then click on those files in the File List window you don't want to back up.

Repeat step 2 for each directory and file you want to deselect. Files are reselected in the same manner.

To Restore Files on a Hard Drive

KEY

1. Press **Alt-R** to display the **R**estore menu.
2. Press **S** to choose the **S**tart Restore command.
3. Insert disks in the disk drive as instructed by the program.
4. You can stop the restoration process at any time by pressing **F3**.

168 PC BACKUP

Shortcut   Press **F6** to start the restoration process.

1. Pull down the Restore menu, and choose the Start Restore command.
2. Insert disks in the disk drive as instructed by the program.
3. You can stop the restoration process at any time by pressing **F3**.

To Save Backup Setup

1. Press **Alt-O** to display the Options menu.
2. Press **S** to choose the Save Setup command.
3. Type a name for the setup file, and press ↵.

Shortcut   Press **Alt-S** to choose the Save Setup command.

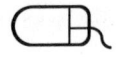

1. Pull down the Options menu, and choose the Save Setup command.
2. Type a name for the setup file, and press ↵.

To Load a File Setup

1. Press **Alt-O** to display the Options menu.
2. Press **L** to choose the Load Setup command.
3. Use the cursor keys to select a setup file, and press ↵.

Shortcut   Press **Alt-L** to choose the Load Setup command.

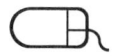

1. Pull down the Options menu, and choose the Load Setup command.
2. Double-click on a setup file, and press ↵.

COMPRESS

• **PURPOSE**   The Compress program defragments files. Over time, files on hard and floppy disks may become fragmented—portions of the files are distributed at nonadjacent points on the surface of the disk. Compress automatically rejoins the files, making disk usage more efficient.

Prior to actually compressing the disk, you can test for file fragmentation and assign the order in which you want the files placed on your disk.

To Start Compress

1. At the DOS prompt, type **COMPRESS**.
2. Press ↵.

To Test for Disk Fragmentation

1. Press **Alt-A** to display the **A**nalysis menu.
2. Press **D** to choose the **D**isk Analysis command.

170 COMPRESS

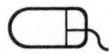

1. Pull down the Analysis menu.
2. Choose the Disk Analysis command.

To Set Order Options

KEY

1. Press **Alt-S** to display the **S**ort menu.
2. Press one of the following keys:
   - **T** to sort by file Date/**T**ime
   - **F** to sort by **F**ile Name
   - **E** to sort by File **E**xtension
   - **S** to sort by File **S**ize
3. Press one of the following keys:
   - **N** for **N**o sorting (the default; previous options ignored)
   - **A** for **A**scending sort (A–Z)
   - **D** for **D**escending sort (Z–A)
4. Press **F3** or **X** to exit the Sort menu.
5. Press **Alt-C** to choose the **C**ompress menu.
6. Press **O** to choose the **O**rdering Options command.
7. Press one of the following:
   - **S** for **S**tandard (files placed on disk in similar order to original; directories first, then files)
   - **.** (period) for .COM & .EXE files first
   - **O** for D**O**S (subs first)—DOS order with subdirectories first, then files
   - **D** for **D**OS (subs w/ files)—DOS order with files and respective subdirectories

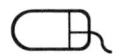

1. Pull down the Sort menu.
2. Click on one of the following:
   - *Date/Time* to sort by file date/time
   - *File Name* to sort by file name
   - *Extension* to sort by file extension
   - *Size* to sort by file size
3. Click on one of the following:
   - *No sorting* (the default; previous options ignored)
   - *Ascending* for A–Z sort
   - *Descending* for Z–A sort
4. Click outside the Sort menu.
5. Pull down the Compress menu, and choose the Ordering Options command.
6. Click on one of the following:
   - *Standard*—for files placed on disk in similar order to original (directories first, then files)
   - *.COM & .EXE files*—executable programs first
   - *DOS (subs first)*—DOS order with subdirectories first, then files
   - *DOS (subs w/ files)*—DOS order with files and respective subdirectories

When using version 5.5, Ordering Options are limited to the following:

- Standard
- DOS (subdirectories first)
- .COM & .EXE first

To Compress a Disk

1. Press **Alt-C** to display the Compress menu.

172 PC FORMAT

2. Press **B** to choose the Begin Compress command.
3. At the warning, press **C** for Continue or **X** for Exit.
4. You can stop disk compression at any time by pressing **F3**.

Shortcut   Press **F4** to choose the Begin Compress command.

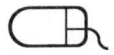

1. Pull down the Compress menu, and choose the Begin Compress command.
2. At the warning, click on the Continue button or Exit button.
3. You can stop disk compression at any time by pressing **F3**.

PC FORMAT

• **PURPOSE**   PC Format is a substitute for the DOS FORMAT command. It provides for greater flexibility and guards against data loss in case of accidental formatting. During installation of the PC Tools files, your original DOS FORMAT command is renamed FORMAT!.COM, and PC Format is named FORMAT.COM.

As with the DOS FORMAT command, PC Format provides a number of formatting options for defining media capacity and format type. Using the PC Format command is an alternative to using the Make Data Disk and Make System Disk commands in the Shell program.

To Start PC Format

1. At the DOS prompt, type **FORMAT** or **PCFORMAT**.
2. Press ↵.

Include one or more of the following options to specify media capacity and format type. These options are typed after the program name at the DOS prompt. Example: **PCFORMAT a:/V**.

PC FORMAT

- **PCFORMAT** starts the PC Format program.
- **a:** selects drive A.
- **/V** instructs the program to prompt for a volume name after formatting is complete.

Different options are available when formatting a floppy or hard disk. The option switches for use with floppy disks are detailed in Table 3.1; only x, /DESTROY, /P, /S, /TEST, and /V are available for formatting hard disks.

Table 3.1: Formatting Options in PC Format

OPTION	FUNCTION
x	Indicates drive to format
/DESTROY	Formats disk and erases it; same as a DOS format (version 6.0 only)
/F	Full format; PC Format reads data on each track, formats tracks, and rewrites same data
/F:nnn	Formats disk with a specific capacity (version 6.0 only)
N:nn	Formats disk with a specified number of sectors per track; used with /T parameter (version 6.0 only)
/P	Prints format information to LPT1 port (version 6.0 only)
/Q	Quick format; erases FAT directory and resets root directory
/R	Reformats and erases every track but leaves FAT and root directory intact
/S	Formats disk and copies system files to disk after formatting is complete
T:nn	Specifies number of tracks to format; used with /N parameter (version 6.0 only)
/TEST	Simulates a format without actually formatting disk (version 6.0 only)

Table 3.1: Formatting Options in PC Format (continued)

OPTION	FUNCTION
/V	Indicates you want to provide volume label for disk after formatting is complete
/1	Formats floppy disk on one side
/4	Formats 360K or 180K disk in 1.2Mb 5¼-inch drive
/8	Formats 360K floppy with 8 sectors per track (1.2Mb with 15)

PC-CACHE

- **PURPOSE** PC-Cache uses the RAM in your computer to store frequently used data from your hard disk. This helps speed up execution of your application programs. The PC-Cache program can use standard (base) RAM, extended RAM, or expanded RAM, in blocks of 64K to 512K.

To Start PC-Cache

1. At the DOS prompt, type **PC-CACHE**.
2. Press ↵.

Include one or more of the following options to specify cache size and other parameters. These options are typed after the program name at the DOS prompt. Example: **PC-CACHE /IA /IB /SIZEXP=256K**.

- **PC-CACHE** starts the PC-Cache program.
- **/IA** ignores caching for the floppy disks in drives A and B.

PC-CACHE 175

- **/IB** instructs the program to use 256K of expanded RAM for the disk cache.

The PC-Cache options are detailed in Table 3.2.

Table 3.2: PC-Cache Options

OPTION	FUNCTION
/Ix	Ignores (does not enable) indicated drive
/SIZE=nnnK	Sets amount of base memory for use by PC-Cache (default is 64K; maximum is 512K)
/SIZEXP=nnnK	Sets amount of expanded memory for use by PC-Cache
/SIZEXT=nnnK	Sets amount of extended memory for use by PC-Cache
/EXT-START=$nnnn$K	Specifies starting address of the cache in extended memory; $nnnn$ must be greater than 1024 (version 6.0 only)
/FLUSH	Empties the cache
/INFO	Displays table of available drives and their sizes, and type and size of cache (version 6.0 only)
/MAX=nn	Specifies maximum number of sectors that can be saved in the cache during a single read request (version 6.0 only)
/MEASURES	Displays relative performance and speed improvements provided by PC-Cache
/PARAM	Displays parameters of PC-Cache currently in effect
/PARAM*	Displays disk usage of memory
/QUIET	Disables sign-on display when PC-Cache first starts (version 6.0 only)

Table 3.2: PC-Cache Options (continued)

OPTION	FUNCTION
/UNLOAD	Clears the cache and unloads PC-Cache from memory
/WRITE=*nn*	Controls time delay before write operations are sent to disk (version 6.0 only)
/?	Displays help on using PC-Cache parameters

MIRROR

- **PURPOSE**   The Mirror program records in a separate file the contents of the file allocation table, root directory, and boot record of your hard disk (Mirror can also be used with floppy drives). This information is critical to the operation of your hard disk and computer; loss of even a byte of data in these areas can cause your hard disk to fail. In case of data loss, the data stored by Mirror can be used by another PC Tools program, Rebuild, to restore the hard disk to its previous condition.

To Run Mirror

1. At the DOS prompt, type **MIRROR**.
2. Press ↵.

To get the best results, include MIRROR in your AUTOEXEC.BAT file so that the program is run every time the computer is started. You may lose important files if you use Rebuild with old Mirror data.

Include one or more of the following options to specify the drive for Mirror backup and other parameters. These options are typed after the program name at the DOS prompt. Example: **MIRROR A: B: C: /TC-256**.

- **MIRROR** starts the Mirror program.
- **A: B: C:** mirrors the file allocation table, directory, and boot record on drives A, B, and C.
- **/TC-256** turns on the delete-tracking option for drive C, with a storage capacity of 256 deleted files.

The Mirror options are the following:

x: indicates the drive you want to mirror. Substitute x for a valid floppy or hard drive, such as A:, B:, or C:. You can include as many drives as you like.

/T selects delete tracking. Delete tracking is a small RAM-resident program that monitors the files you (or your application programs) erase.

/Tx-nnn sets a specific number of entries for delete tracking (up to 256 deleted files); x indicates the drive. Normally, delete tracking holds the maximum number of erased file entries, based on the capacity of the media. The more erased files that are tracked, the larger the delete-tracking file becomes.

REBUILD

- **PURPOSE** Rebuild is used to restore the file allocation table, root directory, and boot block of a damaged disk. The restoration uses the backup file created by the Mirror program.

To Run Rebuild

1. At the DOS prompt, type **REBUILD X:**, where X is the drive you want to reconstruct.
2. Press ↵.

DISKFIX
Version 6.0 Only

- **PURPOSE** Diskfix (version 6.0 only) automatically tests for, and optionally corrects, problems on hard and floppy disks. Diskfix can repair a number of different kinds of disk problems, including lost clusters, missing data, and problems in the file allocation table and root directory. With few exceptions, the program is completely menu-driven, with English-language instructions, prompts, and warnings.

To Run Diskfix

1. At the DOS prompt, type **DISKFIX**.
2. Press ↵.

Diskfix reads the data on your hard drive and makes sure that the critical data on your hard drive are not corrupted. It also checks that your computer and hard-drive mechanism are running properly. These initial checks are necessary so that your disks are not damaged even more by improper repair.

To Fix a Disk

1. Select Yes when Diskfix prompts, "Do you want to repair a disk now?" (Answering No takes you directly to the main menu, step 8.)
2. Select the disk you want to repair.
3. Diskfix checks the following:
   - DOS boot sector
   - Media descriptors
   - File allocation table
   - Directory structure
   - Cross-linked files
   - Lost clusters

If Diskfix spots an error, it prompts you for a course of action, generally to restore or save the damaged data, delete the data, or ignore the error.

4. When main testing is complete, press ↵ to continue.

5. Answer Yes if you want to search for lost directories.

6. Answer Yes if you want to check the media surface.

7. Answer Yes if you want to print a report of analysis results.

8. The main Diskfix action menu appears, with four options:

- Fix a Disk (repeat steps 3 through 8)
- Surface Scan (step 6)
- Revitalize a floppy
- Exit to DOS

PC SECURE

• **PURPOSE** PC Secure is a file security program. It encrypts and decrypts your files so that unauthorized persons can't use or view them. The U.S. version of PC Tools is equipped with an optional Digital Encryption Standard (DES) option for the ultimate in file security. You can also use PC Secure's Standard encryption method, which isn't as secure but takes less time.

To Start PC Secure

1. At the DOS prompt, type **PCSECURE**.

2. Press ↵.

To Encrypt a File

[KEY]

1. Press the **F4** function key.
2. Scroll through the list to find the file you want, or press **Alt-D** to select all the files in a directory.
3. With the file to encrypt highlighted, press **E** for Encrypt.
4. Type a password (up to 32 characters; punctuation is accepted).
5. Press ↵.
6. PC Secure asks you to reenter the password for verification. Repeat the password exactly, and press ↵.
7. PC Secure encrypts the file and displays a status message. Press ↵ to go on.

1. Pull down the File menu, and choose the Encrypt File command.
2. Scroll through the list to find the file you want, or click on the Directory button to select all the files in a directory.
3. With the file to encrypt highlighted, click on the Encrypt button.
4. Type a password (up to 32 characters; punctuation is accepted).
5. Press ↵.
6. PC Secure asks you to reenter the password for verification. Repeat the password exactly, and press ↵.
7. PC Secure encrypts the file and displays a status message. Click on the Exit button to go on.

To Decrypt a File

[KEY]

1. Press the **F5** function key.
2. Scroll through the list to find the file you want, or press **Alt-D** to select all the files in a directory.
3. With the file to decrypt highlighted, press **R** for Encrypt.
4. Type the password (up to 32 characters; punctuation is accepted).
5. Press ↵.
6. PC Secure decrypts the file and displays a status message. Press ↵ to go on.

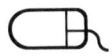

1. Pull down the File menu, and choose the Decrypt File command.
2. Scroll through the list to find the file you want, or click on the Directory button to select all the files in a directory.
3. With the file to decrypt highlighted, click on the Decrypt button.
4. Type the password (up to 32 characters; punctuation is accepted).
5. Press ↵.
6. PC Secure decrypts the file and displays a status message. Click on the Exit button to go on.

● **NOTES** PC Secure allows you to set several options for encrypting and decrypting files. The following commands are on the Options menu:

- Full DES Encryption: encrypts the file by using the DES method, which allows for higher file security but takes a longer time.

- Quick Encryption: encrypts the file by using PC Secure's Standard method.
- Compress: compresses files; use with or without file encryption.
- One key: uses the same password for all files during one session of PC Secure.
- Hidden: encrypts the file and makes it hidden to DOS.
- Read-only: encrypts the file and makes it read-only.
- Delete Original File: encrypts the file and deletes the original.
- Expert Mode: turns Master Key mode on or off. When Expert Mode is selected, Master Key mode is off; the master key you entered when you first configured PC Secure is not used for file encryption, and you cannot decrypt the file by using the master password.
- Save Preferences: saves option settings.

Appendix A

START-UP OPTIONS FOR SHELL AND DESKTOP

The options described below are available when starting Shell and Desktop or can be added to the command line at the DOS prompt.

Option	Function
A*nnn*	Allocates *nnn* K of RAM when Shell is loaded in RAM-resident mode
/BW	Starts in black-and-white mode
/DQ	Disables quick-load feature
/FF	Disables screen-snow suppression
/F*n*	Changes default hotkey (substitute *n* for Ctrl key)
/LCD	Starts in mono mode for laptop LCD screens; use to set colors (version 6.0 only)
/LE	Exchanges right and left mouse buttons
/IM	Disables mouse
/IN	Hercules InColor graphics mode
/MM	Starts Desktop without invoking a Desktop application that may have been running during the last session (Desktop and version 6.0 only)
/O*d*	Selects drive for overlay files (substitute *d* with desired drive)
/350	350-line mode for VGA monitors
/PS2	Resets IBM PS/2 mouse (version 6.0 only)
/R	RAM-resident mode (default)
/RT	RAM-resident mode; tiny (uses about 10K of RAM)

/RS	RAM-resident mode; small (uses about 117K of RAM)
/RM	RAM-resident mode; medium (uses about 155K of RAM)
/RL	RAM-resident mode; large (uses about 235K of RAM)
/TRn	Updates directory tree every n days

Appendix B

PC TOOLS PROGRAM FILES

The following are the major files used by PC Tools Deluxe. Files are applicable to both versions 5.5 and 6.0, unless otherwise noted.

GENERAL FILES

File	Function
PCSETUP.COM	PC Setup program
KILL.EXE	Removes Shell and Desktop when installed as RAM-resident program

SHELL FILES

File	Function
PCRUN.COM	Shell run-time module; runs other programs while in Shell
PCSHELL.EXE	Main Shell program
PCSHELL.HLP	Shell help
PCSHELL.OVL	Shell message overlay
PCSHELL.CFG	Shell configuration

DESKTOP FILES

File	Function
DESKTOP.EXE	Main Desktop program
DESKTOP.HLP	Desktop help
ASCII.OVL	ASCII table utility overlay
CALC.OVL	Algebraic calculator module overlay
DBMS.OLV	Database module overlay
FAX1.OVL	Fax communications overlay (6.0)

File	Function
FAX2.OVL	Fax communications overlay (6.0)
FINCALC.OVL	Financial calculator module overlay
HEXCALC.OVL	Hexadecimal calculator module overlay
HOTKEY.OVL	Hotkey utility overlay
INKILL.OVL	Desktop program remover utility overlay
MACROS.OVL	Macro editor overlay
RECOLOR.OVL	Screen color utility overlay
SPELL.OVL	Spelling checker (Notepads) overlay
TALK.OVL	Telecom module overlay
TIME.OVL	Appointment calendar module overlay
BACKTALK.EXE	Background communications program
DICT.SPL	Spelling dictionary (Notepads)
PHONE.TEL	Phone directory (Telecommunications)

UTILITY FILES

File	Function
COMPRESS.EXE	Compress program
COMPRESS.HLP	Compress help
COMPRESS.CFG	Compress configuration
MIRROR.COM	Mirror program
MIRROR.FIL	Mirror system image
MIRROR.BAK	Backup (old copy) of Mirror system image
MIRORSAV.FIL	Mirror pointer file
PCTRACKR.DEL	Mirror delete-tracking file
PARTNSAV.FIL	Mirror partition table image
REBUILD.COM	Rebuild program
PC-CACHE.COM	PC-Cache program
PCFORMAT.COM	PC Format program
PCSECURE.EXE	PC Secure program

File	Function
PCSECURE.HLP	PC Secure help
PCSECURE.CFG	PC Secure configuration

BACKUP FILES

File	Function
PCBACKUP.EXE	PC Backup main program
PCBACKUP.HLP	PC Backup help
PCBACKUP.CFG	PC Backup configuration
PCB1.EXE	PC Backup file
PCB2.EXE	PC Backup file
PCB3.EXE	PC Backup file
PCB4.EXE	PC Backup file
PCB5.EXE	PC Backup file
PCB6.EXE	PC Backup file
PCBDIR.COM	Disk identification program (5.5)
<name>.SET	PC Backup setup files

SUPPORT FILES

File	Function
<script>.SCR	Script file for Telecommunications (includes CompuServe, MCI, and Easylink)
<printer>.PRO	Printer function macro (for Epson, IBM, Panasonic, and HP printers)
<file>.TXT	Sample Notepads and Outlines documents
<file>.FOR	Sample Databases form documents
<file>.DBF	Sample Databases documents
<file>.VWR	Shell viewer filter files (6.0)
DISKFIX.EXE	Diskfix program (6.0)

File	Function
FAX.PHO	Fax phone number file (6.0)
LLQC.EXE	LapLink QC program (6.0)
ITLFAX.	Fax communications program (6.0)
MEMCHK.COM	Memory-checking program
MI.COM	Memory-mapping program
PARK.COM	Disk-parking utility
PC-CACHE.SYS	PC-Cache .SYS file
UNDELETE.EXE	Stand-alone file undelete program (6.0)
VIEWERS.EXE	File viewers program (6.0)
README.TXT	Additions and updates to documentation
SAMPLE.<ext>	Sample Desktop application documents

Index

Active List Switch, 2–3
active programs, memory blocks for, 66
active windows
  changing, 2
  switching between Tree and File List windows, 107–108
Advanced user level, 8–9, 96
Algebraic Calculator, 161
application programs, searching for document files belonging to, 63
Applications menu, adding and removing programs on, 67–71
Appointment Scheduler (Desktop), 158–161
  changing displayed date in, 160–161
archive file attribute, 3, 6
ASCII files
  editing, 37–38
  viewing, 20–21, 82, 116–117
Attribute Change, 3–6
attributes of directories, 25, 30
attributes of files, 3–6, 74
AUTOEXEC.BAT file, Mirror program in, 176
Autosave feature, in Notepads, 131

Background Mat, 6–7, 96
backup files, 187
backup process, xiii
  for all files, 166
  and archive attribute, 3
  restoring files after, 167–168
bad clusters, sectors for, 34
bad sectors, 33, 54
batch files, running from PC Shell, 60–61, 89–90
Beginning user level, 8–9, 96
binary files
  editing, 55–58
  printing, 79–81
  viewing, 82, 116–117
binary hexadecimal format, displaying files in, 20–21
BIOS program date, 101
boot record
  restoring to damaged disk, 177
  sectors for, 34
  storing record of, 176–177
bootable disks, 54
Borland Quattro, viewing files from, 84

Calculators (Desktop), 161–162
calendar, 158
Change Drive, 7–8
Change User Level, 8–9
Clear File, 9–10
clicking mouse, xiv
Clipboard (Desktop), 163
Clipper, viewing files from, 84
clock in system, 5–6
  setting date and time on, 18–20
clusters, 33
  bad, 34
  display of, 48
  for files, 74
  lost, 178
colors, on screen display, 91–94
COM ports, 132
communications
  by fax, 156–158
  hard-wired link for, 59–60
  by modem, 152–156
Compare. *See* Compare File
Compare Disk, 11–12
Compare File, 13–14
Compress program, 169–172
computer type, 101
Copy. *See* Copy File
Copy Disk, 14–16
Copy File, 16–18
copying text, in Notepads, 132–133
CPU type, 101
Ctrl-↵ key combination, 90
  for Launch command, 61
cutting text, in Notepads, 132–133
cylinders, 33

Daily diary, 158
data recovery, xii, xiii, 111–112
Databases (Desktop), 142–152
  adding new record to, 148
  creating new file for, 144–145

deleting record from, 148
editing in, 143–146
Goto command in, 151
loading existing forms in, 146–147
opening, 143
printing in, 147–148
searching for text string in, 150–151
selecting records in, 149
sorting in, 150
date, changing in Appointment Scheduler, 160–161
date of files, modifying, 3–6
Date/Time, 18–20, 97
dBASE files, viewing, 82, 84
.DBF file-name extensions, 142, 144
dBXL, viewing files from, 84
Default Viewer, 20–21, 83, 97
Define Function Keys, 21–23
Delete. *See* Delete File
Delete File, 23–24
Delete Tracking option, 112
deleting subdirectories, 27–28
Desktop, 125–163
 Appointment Scheduler, 158–161
 Calculators, 161–162
 Clipboard, 163
 Databases, 142–152
 Fax Telecommunications, 156–158
 files for, 185–186
 Macro Editor, 162
 Modem Telecommunications, 152–156
 Notepads, 127–141
 Outlines, 141–142
 starting, 126
 start-up options for, 183–184
dialog boxes, colors of, 91–94
Digital Encryption Standard (DES), 179
DIP switches, settings on, 100
directories. *See also* root directory
 changing attributes of, 30
 creating, 25–26
 deleting, 27–28
 disk space for, 33
 displaying contents of, 76–78
 displaying tree for current drive, 7–8
 forcing PC Shell to reread, 88
 maintaining, 25–30
 moving files between, 74–76
 printing file list from, 81–82
 pruning and grafting, 29
 renaming, 26–27

Directory Maint, 25–30
Directory Sort, 31–32
disk drives
 changing current, 7–8, 28
 number of logical, 101
Disk File option, for Notepads printing, 132
Disk Info, 32–34
Disk Initialization dialog box, 53
Disk Map, 34–35
Disk View window, commands for, 119
Diskfix program, xiii, 178–179
disks. *See also* floppy disks; hard disks
 comparing, 11–12
 displaying contents of, 76–78
 fragmentation test on, 169–170
 relative location of file on, 47
 searching for text string on, 94–96
 total space on, 33
 verifying integrity of, 114–115
 volume label for, 52, 87–88
DisplayWrite, viewing files from, 84
document files, viewing, 82, 116–117
DOS Command Line, 36–37, 96
DOS commands
 FORMAT, 52, 172
 pause after, 122
DOS Dir method, for undeleting files, 112
DOS operating system
 memory used by, 102
 returning to, 39–40
double-clicking mouse, xv
drag copying files, 17–18
drag moving files, 75–76
dragging mouse, xv

Edit File, 37–39
 vs. Hex Edit File, 58
editing
 in Databases, 143–146
 of hexadecimal notation, 55–58
 in Notepads, 127–130
erased files, 23–24
 null characters to replace, 9–10
 recovering, xiii, 111–112
 searching, 94–96
Excel, viewing files from, 84
Exit PC Shell, 39–40
exiting, Notepads, 132
expanded memory, 102
extended memory, 102

Fax Telecommunications (Desktop), 156–158
fields, naming, 145
file allocation table (FAT)
  restoring to damaged disk, 177
  sectors for, 34
  storing record of, 176–177
  testing, 178
File Display Options, 40–43, 51
File Edit. *See* Edit File
File List Filter, 43–46, 51
File List Window, 46–47, 76, 109
  changing selection parameters for, 49–51
  deselecting files in, 113–114
  display in, 41–43
  display parameters for, 44–46
  hiding window, 59
  switching between Tree and, 107–108
File Map, 47–49
File Select Filter, 43, 49–51
file-name extensions
  .DBF, 142, 144
  .TXT, 128
files. *See also* backup process; erased files
  attributes of, 3–6, 74
  comparing contents of, 13–14
  copying, 16–18
  creating in Notepads, 128
  defragmenting, 169–172
  displaying, 20–21, 116–117
  displaying information about, 73–74
  editing, 37–39
  editing with Notepads, 127–130
  encryption and decryption of, 179–182
  forcing PC Shell to reread, 88
  fragmented, 47, 169–172
  list of, 7–8
  modifying attributes, date or time of, 3–6
  moving to different directory, 74–76
  printing contents of, 79–81
  printing list of, 81–82
  receiving with modem, 155
  renaming, 86–87
  restoring from backup copies, 167
  searching for text string in, 61–64, 102–107
  sectors for, 34
  sending through modem, 154–155
  verifying integrity of, 116

Financial Calculator, 161
Find. *See* Text Search
floppy disks
  bootable, 54
  formatting, 52–54
  making copy of, 14–16
  system, 64–65
  testing, 178–179
footers
  in Notepads, 139
  printing, 80
form letters, 142
Format Data Disk, 52–54
forms, loading existing, in Databases, 146–147
FoxBASE, viewing files from, 84
fragmented files, 47
  compressing, 169–172
function keys, redefining, 21–23, 97

Goto command
  in Databases, 151
  in Notepads, 134

Hard disks. *See also* backup process
  archival program for, 166–169
  crash of, 78
  parking heads of, 78
  restoring files to, 167–168
  testing, 178–179
hardware, xiv
hard-wired communications link, 59–60
headers
  in Notepads, 139
  printing, 80
Headlines menu, 141–142
heads of hard disks, parking, 78
Hex Edit. *See* Hex Edit File
Hex Edit File, 55–58
hexadecimal notation
  for file editing, 55–58
  printing files in, 80
  viewing files in, 83
hidden files
  attribute for, 3
  disk space for, 33
Hide Windows, 58–59
hooked vectors, 67

Indents, 140
Ins key, 77
Intermediate user level, 8–9, 96

LapLink/QC, 59–60
laptop computers
 connecting to, 59–60
 setting display for, 94
Launch, 60–61
line spacing, in Notepads, 138
Load Setup command, 168–169
Locate File, 61–64
logical disk drives, number of, 101
lost clusters, repairing, 178
Lotus 1-2-3 files, viewing, 82, 84
Lotus Symphony, viewing files from, 84
LPT port, 132

Macro Editor (Desktop), 162
Make Data Disk, 172
Make System Disk, 54, 64–65, 172
margins
 in Notepads, 138
 for printing, 80
math coprocessor, 102
memory, 102
 loaded programs in, 65–67
Memory Map, 65–67
memory-resident software. *See* terminate-and-stay-resident programs
menus
 colors of, 91–94
 hiding, 58–59
 for shortcut keys, 98–99
message boxes, colors of, 91–94
Microsoft Word, viewing files from, 84
Microsoft Works, viewing files from, 84
Mirror program, xiii, 112, 176–177
Modem Telecommunications (Desktop), 152–156
 entering settings for, 153–154
 hanging up the phone in, 154
 opening, 152–153
 placing call in, 154
 receiving file with, 155
 sending files with, 154–155
Modify Applications List, 67–71
Modify Display, 71–72
monthly calendar, 158
More File Info, 67, 73–74
Mosaic Twin, viewing files from, 84
motherboard BIOS chip, 101
mouse, xiv–xv
Move. *See* Move File
Move File, 74–76
moving mouse pointer, xiv

moving windows, 99–100
MultiMate, viewing files from, 84
MultiPlan, viewing files from, 84

Notepads (Desktop), 127–141
 creating files in, 128
 cutting, copying, and pasting text in, 132–133
 deleting text in, 133
 document display in, 140–141
 editing file with, 127–130
 exiting, 132
 finding text in, 135–136
 Goto command in, 134
 headers and footers in, 139
 inserting file into current document, 134
 loading document in, 129–130
 opening, 127
 page layout in, 138
 printing from, 131–132
 saving current setup, 140
 saving document in, 130–131
 searching and replacing text in, 136–137
 spelling check in, 134–135
 tab ruler in, 139–140
null characters, to replace erased file, 9–10
null-modem cable, 60

One List Display, 13, 76–78
operating system, 101
Ordering Options (Compress program), 170–171
Outlines (Desktop), 141–142
Overtype mode, 140

Page numbers, for printing, 80
Paradox, viewing files from, 84
parallel ports, 101
Park Disk, 78
password, 180
pasting text, in Notepads, 132–133
PC Backup, 166–172
PC-Cache, 174–176
PC Format, 54, 172–174
PC Secure, 179–182
PC Shell, xii, xiii, 1–123
 customizing, 96–98
 DOS command line in, 36–37
 exiting, 39–40

files for, 185
function keys in, 22–23
modifying display appearance, 71–72
printing with options from, 80
reactivating after DOS command, 122
retaining in RAM, 85–86
running programs from, 60–61, 89–90
saving configuration settings for, 91
start-up options for, 183–184
PC Tools Deluxe, xii–xiv
  program files for, 185–188
PCSHELL.CFG file, 23
Phone Directory window, 153
ports. *See* parallel ports; serial ports
Print Directory. *See* Print File List
Print File, 79–81
Print File List, 81–82
printing
  from Databases, 147–148
  from Notepads, 131–132
program files, 185–188
program memory blocks, 66–67
Programmer's Calculator, 161
programs
  adding to Applications menu, 67–69
  deleting from Applications menu, 70–71
  editing Applications menu listing, 69–70
  files for PC Tools, 185–188
  listing those in memory, 65–67
  loaded, memory location for, 102
  running from PC Shell, 60–61, 89–90
pull-down menus, xiii

uick File View, 82–84
Quick Run, 85–86, 90

RAM (random access memory), xiv
  keeping PC Shell in, 85–86
  loaded programs in, 65–67
  PC-Cache and, 174–176
R:BASE, viewing files from, 84
read-only files
  attribute for, 3
  sectors for, 34
Rebuild program, xiii, 177
recovery of erased files, 111–112
relative speed of computer, 101
remote computer, hard-wiring to, 59–60
Rename. *See* Rename File
Rename File, 86–87

Rename Volume, 87–88
renaming subdirectories, 26–27
Re-Read the Tree, 88
Reset button, 45, 50
Reset Selected Files. *See* Unselect Files
resident mode, PC Shell in, 85–86
restoring files, from backup copies, 167–168
root directory
  restoring to damaged disk, 177
  storing record of, 176–177
  testing, 178
Run, 89–90

Save Configuration. *See* Save Configuration File
Save Configuration File, 91
Save Setup command, 168
Scientific Calculator, 161
Screen Colors, 91–94, 97
Search Disk, 94–96
sectors, 33
  bad, 33, 54
  displaying contents of, 118–119
serial ports, 101
Setup Configuration, 6, 96–98
SETUP parameters, display of, 100
Shell. *See* PC Shell
shortcut keys, display of, 96
Short Cut Keys command, 98–99
Size/Move Window, 99–100
sorting
  in Databases, 150
  in File List Window, 41–43
  files in directory, 31–32
spelling check, in Notepads, 134–135
string. *See* text string search
subdirectories. *See* directories
support files, 187–188
system attribute, 6
system clock, 5–6
  setting, 18–20
system disks, creating, 64–65
system file attribute, 3
System Info, 100–102

Tab ruler
  display of, 140
  in Notepads, 139–140
telecommunications. *See*
  Fax Telecommunications;
  Modem Telecommunications

terminate-and-stay-resident programs
  Desktop as, 125
  memory blocks for, 66
  memory used by, 102
Text Search, 102–107
text string search
  in Databases, 150–151
  of disk, 94–96
  of files, 61–64, 102–107
  in Notepads, 135–136
  and replace, in Notepads, 136–137
tiling of windows, 120
time of files, modifying, 3–6
to-do list, 158, 160
tracks, 33
  formatting, 54
Tree/File List windows, switching, 2–3
Tree/Files Switch, 107–108
Tree List Window, 108–109
  hiding window, 59
Tree window, 76, 109
Two List Display, 2, 109–110
.TXT file-name extensions, 128

Undelete. *See* Undelete Files, 110
Undelete Files, 111–112
Unselect Files, 113–114
user files, disk space for, 33
user interface, xiii–xiv
user level, changing, 8–9, 96
utility files, 186–187

Vectors, hooked, 67
Verify. *See* Verify File
Verify Disk, 114–115
Verify File, 115–116

video adapter, 102
View, 116–117
View/Edit Disk, 118–119
View Window, 121
  orientation of, 96
Viewer Cfg., 96, 120–121
volume names for disks, 52
  changing, 87–88
VP Planner Plus, viewing files from, 84

Wait on DOS Screen, 37, 96, 122
wildcards, to limit file display, 44
Window menu, and Notepads
  document display, 141
windows
  arrangement of, 120
  changing active, 2
  colors of, 91–94
  hiding, 58–59
  moving and resizing, 99–100
  tiling, 120
  zooming, 123
Windows Write, viewing files from, 84
word processor. *See* Notepads
WordPerfect, viewing files from, 84
Words and Figures, viewing files from, 84
WordStar files
  editing, 37–38
  viewing, 84
word-wrap, 140

XMODEM command, 155–156
XyWrite, viewing files from, 84

Zoom the Current Window, 123